Seeing Through Blindness

Matt Harris

authorHOUSE®

AuthorHouse™
1663 Liberty Drive
Bloomington, IN 47403
www.authorhouse.com
Phone: 1-800-839-8640

Dates, places, and events in this story are factual. Some fictional names were invented, and some details altered, to protect the privacy of those who were actually involved. Composites from several different people were also created to further protect privacy and to help move the narrative along.

To book Matt for a speaking and reciting engagement, or to discuss his book, please contact him at matt@harrispoems.com. For more information about his other books, please visit www.harrispoems.com.

Published by AuthorHouse   01/31/2013

ISBN: 978-1-4817-0736-7 (sc)
ISBN: 978-1-4817-0737-4 (e)

Library of Congress Control Number: 2013900880

To My Beautiful Wife,

Pam,

My Best Friend and Right Hand;

And To My Lovely Daughters,

Julia & Abigail

Contents

Part One, Retinitis Pigmentosa (RP)

Allow me to introduce you to the beast
I once was, before I became this
new creature through the blood of God's Son.
Come and travel down the stairs of time with me,
but first, watch your step, and grab the railing please,
until we alight on the landing dated
August 21, 1981,
where I'll begin this tale of my dark daze
of drug abuse, blindness, and rebellion,
through which the Light of the world would shine on me!

"Matt Harris, Dr. Miller can see you now,"
my eye doctor's assistant tells me,
her pupils peeking over glasses set low
on her nose. For days, I'd already been
waiting, like a defendant for a verdict,
for the test results to determine why
my eyes had been so uncooperative
for the past ten years . . . since age eleven.

"Have a seat, Matt." Dr. Miller says.
"Your test results confirm what we discussed
on your initial visit with me.
You have Retinitis Pigmentosa—
or RP for short. It's incurable
and progressive, and, so far, has carved
eighty-two degrees from your visual field,
which puts you in the legally blind range—though

1

your acuity is still 20/20."

Dr. Miller diagnosed in ten minutes
what doctors for the past decade had missed!

Later that day, I surrender my cares.
Sliding an eight-track tape into its player,
"Born to be Wild" by Steppenwolf stirs,
as the third hit of weed from my bong explodes
inside my lungs. Immediately,
tentacles from THC tickle my brain,
as it cuts a swath through my synapses.
My black bucket seat absorbs me inside
the refuge of my '68 *Mustang,*
its Firestones eagerly awaiting
to leave their marks on asphalt once again,
rather than idling in its current state,
sinking into leaves and twigs from oak trees,
that stand as stoic sentries to its prison:
the tangled woods behind my parents' house.
And although I've not driven my black beauty
for two years, still, whenever I clench the wheel,
and my key turns the engine into music,
in my imagination, I travel to
the outermost dimensions of my choosing.

My lack of funds is the excuse I use
to tell people why my *Mustang* has sat
corralled in the woods for the past two years.
The truth is I could not lie anymore,

at least not to myself, about the fact
that my eyes had become like sponges,
and some unknown entity had been wringing
peripheral vision from their field. Yet,
lying about it comforts me more than truth—
a weapon I learned to use to survive.
For a falsehood to convince, it commands
certain manipulative dexterities:
the two most essential skills for success are
a swift mind and a memory of stone,
upon which to chisel each fable on:
a data bank for future reference.

After my bong strikes me with two more hits,
torment chafes my mind over the thought of how
my memories are oftentimes much like
a burning building with me trapped inside.
As smoke begins to overwhelm me again,
I remember a time long ago, when,
even before my first RP symptom
pitched its tent to camp in my visual field,
white lies in my defective cones distorted
my own perception of what color was.
My parents told my fourth-grade teacher, Sister
Agnes Marie, about my colorblindness.
She promised to help and not to tell a soul.
But just like how air escapes from the mouth
of a balloon, so, too, my secret leaked.
A bully at recess named Joseph Sear
chose to deride me in front of some kids:

"What color's this, blind as a bat Matt,"
he teased, while holding up different objects,
as other children joined in the fun with him.
Ashamed, I yelled and lied, "I'm not colorblind."
And when he refused to stop, I showed him
how bullies bleed just like the rest of us.
(Grandma taught me *that* when I was but four,
when a kid busted my lip with a swing
at a park in Curtis Bay. She grabbed me
and half dragged me to the drinking fountain,
where he had run to splash kids with some water.
"Take your fist, Matt," Grandma said, "and bash him
in the mouth." I always listened to Grandma.)
After I bashed Joseph Sear with my fist,
I would have sworn his blood looked brown to me.
And though Joseph Sear never asked me,
what the color of something was again,
he became what most fallen bullies become:
a *victim*. After squealing like a school girl
to Sister Agnes Marie, that I'd hit him,
and that I'd lied about my colorblindness,
she hit me with a punch harder than any
that a playground bully could have mustered.
In front of my fourth grade class, she tested me
to see if I was *really* colorblind.
Clenching her wooden pointer, she waddled
to the bulletin board, where hot air balloons,
our class had fashioned from construction paper,
hung lazily, stapled to the sky.
"What color is this one, Matt?" She asked,

while tapping her pointer on a balloon.
"And don't lie!" My ears burned with an anger
that would be my unwelcomed guest for years.
"Joseph made fun of me. That's why I lied,"
I cried, the balloons blurring through my tears.

I put so much time and money into
my Mustang. And for what? I ask myself,
as I replace Steppenwolf with Fleetwood Mac,
and space out on the smoke that rises
from the half inch of ash that quivers
on my *Salem,* lounging in its ashtray,
as if it has answers to some mystery.
While I chew on my diagnosis,
like a piece of Wrigley's *Doublemint Gum,*
this epiphany floods me with some relief:
For the first time in ten years I know
what my problem is. Why is that funny?
If I had a belly, it would be jiggling!
I can't stop laughing. Why would I want to?
Is it the pot? No! It's this paradox:
a blind man with 20/20 vision!
Thunder only happens when it's raining,
Fleetwood Mac says, smoothing out my buzz a bit.
My thunder started when I was eleven;
that's when symptoms from my RP first started.

* * *

Part Two, Diamond Daze

I'd heard how diamonds were a girl's best friend, but
when I was a boy, living in Baltimore,
I played inside a diamond so much so
that it became one of my very best friends,
as it encompassed me with all its brilliance.
In the neighborhood, we seldom were apart.
For years already, by age 11,
baseball had been like a brother to me.
Even the bios on backs of baseball cards
tutored me in reading like a teacher,
resulting in a savant-like knowledge of
hundreds of players' batting averages,
ERAs, RBIs, and homerun totals.

It was spring, 1971. Yes!
And the Orioles were World Series champions,
having clobbered Cincinnati in the fall.
I grabbed my ball glove and bike and pedaled
over the coarse concrete that wended its way
through blocks of bleak blue-collar brick row homes.
Old Bay seasoning, coating crabs while they steamed,
clawed at my nose, as its scent streamed through screened doors.
Hurried women hung wet wash on their clotheslines,
white linens waving like flags of surrender,
while, with a *Pabst* in one hand, and a *Pall Mall*
burning in the other, men rested
their tired forearms on chain-linked fences, talking
and laughing more loudly with each emptied *Pabst*.

This was home, the aroma of Lakeland.

As I steered my bike with its extended forks
into the park, drifting toward the diamond,
at ease on my brand new banana seat,
I heard that *screech*, a musical note to me,
when the barrel of an aluminum bat
introduced itself to a baseball,
and the applause that always followed,
either for the batter, when he reached base,
or for the fielder, when he threw him out.
The word *exhilaration* did not exist
in my decade-old vocabulary
back in '71; but now I know
it expressed how baseball once whirled inside me.

After chaining my bike to a lamppost,
I sneezed when I smelled the freshly cut grass
that pieced together our little league field.
"*Gesundheit*, Duck," my teammate, Nicholas, said,
hustling out to field his first-base position.
We played on the same all-star squad last year,
where I'd gobbled up everything hit my way
at second base. I'd never felt more at home.
When practice started this year, that all changed,
as groundballs rolled unnoticed right by me;
I moved for line drives only when they hit me.
And when pop up after pop up started
to descend like aerial assaults, they would
occasionally plunk me in the head,

7

which eventually conditioned me to duck.
And, of course, more often than not, the batter
hit the ball elsewhere. And I'd still be ducking.
And, so, my teammates started calling me *Duck*.
I had no humor about it at all then;
in fact, their laughter knocked the wind from me
harder than an errant fastball to the back.
And just like how I battled to see a ball,
once it was launched from a baseball bat,
the eye doctors, my parents would take me to
over the next decade, also struggled
to diagnose my difficulty.

As opening day festivities began,
armies of families from the neighborhood
gathered with lounge chairs and charcoal grills,
that hurled their pleasant, scented gusts from scores
of hamburgers, *Esskay Franks*, and chicken legs,
while their envied juices trickled to the coals.
I found my niche, the bench, and stuck to it,
like the *P* on my cap that stood for Phillies.
I was becoming an outcast, more and more,
though still confident my problem would soon pass.
Maybe today I'll see the ball better,
I mused, after my coach, Mr. Don, yelled,
"Matt, since Chester ain't here yet, you're starting
in right field and you'll be batting ninth."
And though I'd been deported that year
from second base, and exiled to right field,
and fell from batting leadoff to hitting ninth,

nothing at that time could compare to
the feel of my sweaty fingers inside
the threadbare glove secured to my left hand.
Armed to the teeth with several pieces of
Bazooka Bubble Gum, I worked my molars
and my mandible, while bubbles bloomed and popped,
until the umpire shouted, *Play Ball!*
Our pitcher threw wildly, walking the first
three batters in a row on 12 straight pitches.
When Lou, batting cleanup, lumbered to the plate,
I began to pray, "Dear God, please don't
let him hit the ball my way. But God said *No*
to my prayer and *Yes* to Lou Paul's instead.
Connecting with a gift our pitcher threw,
aluminum squealed *Hello* to the ball.
Deep to right, the blast sailed over my head;
I never saw it—not even a glimpse.
I heard it, though, rattle the rusty fence,
so I scanned its grassy bottom with my eyes.
I squinted and squinted, as Nicholas,
our first baseman, ran passed me. Shaking his head,
he howled through clenched teeth, glinting with braces,
"You moron! What the heck's your problem, Matt?"
"Wish I knew," I said. As he hurled the ball home,
the bases had emptied. Four runs had scored.
When Nicholas' gloved-hand struck my head,
it didn't hurt as much as the din
of laughter from the stands. So, there, in right field,
I swallowed my gum, my pride, and stood alone
like a blade of grass about to be mown.

An edge of hardness started sharpening
itself on a whetstone inside me—too
intangible then for me to have dulled it.
Nonetheless that *edge* began in a diamond,
hacking away at me like a madman
slashing a turkey's carcass on Thanksgiving—
more than a baseball disappeared that day.

*   *   *

Part Three, Still in the Mustang

Are magicians on the loose in my *Mustang?*
More than my eyesight seems to be vanishing.
Because after my last bong hit, my reefer
disappeared, as well as my *Doritos!*
Jeeter, my *pharmacist,* referred to it
as *Gungi Weed.* Jeeter bought a boatload,
metaphorically speaking, of course,
from some dreadlocked Jamaican dude new to town.
But any pothead worth a buzz always has
a stash to counter such acts of vanishing.
A favorite feature on my *Mustang* is
how easily the cover at the center
of the steering wheel pries away, exposing
a cylinder hidden behind it, in which
I can store a spare supply of pot.
I wonder if Ford engineered this nifty
design to serve for such a purpose as this!

I'm not surprised how RP has taken
its twisted finger and poked me in each eye.
Yet I had no idea my eyesight languished
in such an impoverished state as this.
It answers one question that has hounded me,
like a pit bull chasing a Chihuahua:
No! I've not been crazy for the past decade,
and, still, many would have a sound argument
to the contrary. But, now, at least,
documentation exists as to why,

like an out-of-shape runner at a track meet,
striving breathlessly to keep pace with the pack,
I've lagged behind my peers for ten years now,
academically, athletically,
socially, and vocationally.
Yet, ironically, liberation
lifts me like a man just freed from prison,
since my blindness can now be defined this day—
August 21, 1981—
which reminds me the O's and A's are playing,
with Jim Palmer and Rick Langford on the mound.

And no more *Rumors* from you, Fleetwood Mac.
Yes! I'm pulling the plug on that "Don't Stop"
crap! It sounds like a broken record,
after listening to it a dozen times:

If you wake up and don't want to smile,
If it takes just a little while,
Open your eyes and look at the day,
You'll see things in a different way.

Don't stop, thinking about tomorrow,
Don't stop, it'll soon be here,
It'll be, better than before,
Yesterday's gone, yesterday's gone.
Why not think about times to come,
And not about the things that you've done,
If your life was bad to you,
Just think what tomorrow will do . . . .

Okay, let's see, now, what will tomorrow do?
Bring me a day closer to complete darkness?
Or bring me a guide dog I can call *Buddy?*
Or even better yet, I know, how 'bout this:
a white cane in my hand to travel behind
to keep my dumb butt from bumping into stuff?
And how will I buy dope, much less feed *Buddy,*
when I join the unemployment club?
Yep, that's what *my* tomorrow will do!

But for today, I'll crack open a can
of ice-cold *Budweiser* from my cooler
to conquer my cotton mouth and wash away
the fuzz that clings to the walls of my throat.
Aah! There's my *Doritos,* right next to me,
hiding on the floor. Mmm! Nothing cures
my munchies like handfuls of *Doritos.*
What's up with this stupid static? I'm gonna
miss the first pitch. *Bash the dash.* Bam! Yep,
that always gets her tuned in real nice.
"No score after one," Chuck Thompson announces.
Stupid realtor commercial. I hate it!
It reminds me of when we moved from Lakeland
to the boondocks out here in Pasadena.

*   *   *

Part Four, At Home

Nestled on Norland Road, between hundreds
like it, in the midst of Lakeland, our row home,
I revered, since age three, sheltered me,
my mom, dad, and little sister, Cindy.
The candles on my fourteenth birthday cake
had only been snuffed out for a few months,
when the words *FOR SALE*, blasting like neon
from its *Doyle Realty* sign, blared at me
from its stake stabbed in the heart of my front yard.
I flipped my *Salem* at the smiling face
of the pretty woman plastered on the sign.
She took a direct hit to the forehead—
at least my aim was still on target.

After bicycling to the local store,
I tossed 42 cents on the counter,
and snatched my cigarettes and some matches,
then pushed through the door of 7/11.
Before hopping back onto my bike,
I had to wait a few minutes, as always,
till the sun stopped suppressing my eyesight.
This *whiteout* occurred each time I exited
any building. And also, when I entered
into any building, my eyesight
called for a *timeout*, while waiting in darkness,
till they adjusted to the inside lighting.
Whiteouts and *timeouts* lasted for minutes,
and, of course, they were as foreign as French

to my friends, so frustration filled me, like
a rookie batting against Nolan Ryan,
when I lost step with them, while leaving,
or going into, houses, stores, or school.
I was falling behind in an ever-
widening gap in a race with my peers.

In sync with the sun once again, I flew
across the parking lot, looking straight forward,
on a day more clear than plain English.
My handlebars rocked me in my ribcage,
like a solid left hook to the body,
as I crashed into the concrete wheel-stop
at the edge of a parking space, directly
in front of the Pantry Pride Supermarket.
My bicycle catapulted me headlong!
As I belly-flopped onto the black surface,
the sultry asphalt slapped me in the face.
After skidding to a stop like a Goodyear,
I was in a pile of pain, like an untrained
fighter on the canvas down for the count.
Lacerations tattooed me from face to feet,
while my flesh sizzled from the road burn,
like a French fry dipped in a deep fryer.
As I straightened my twisted handlebars,
my abrasions throbbed with every heartbeat,
while the polio of apathy hobbled
the hamstrings of slews of consumers, who,
ignorant of the term *Good Samaritan*,
begged off treading anywhere near my plight.

With another embarrassment behind me,
I lit my smoke and slung my match to the wind,
driving gingerly to the park, careful
not to allow any more *bumps* upend me,
that, perhaps, my naked eye would not detect.
I had not been blinded to the fact
how I needed to concentrate more and more
to see, as less and less came into view.
And while this mystery speckled torment
throughout every region of my psyche,
my suffering alone in this manner
weighed down on me like a blacksmith's anvil.
As I attempted to forge a solution
to my ophthalmological problem,
that had just recently stumped the world famous
Wilmer Eye Institute at Johns Hopkins,
I drifted and entered into the park,
standing to pedal faster passed the diamond,
wishing the memory it still conjured up—
that fly ball three years ago I flubbed—
would crumble like clay I once kicked from my cleats.
I pulled in the basketball court, which smelled
like ammonia from us boys using its walls
as urinals during our basketball games.
"Hey Jeeter, pass me the ball," I said.
Since age three, Jeeter Jones and I have been friends.
Right after we met, a piece of brick tested
our friendship. While acting like three-year-olds,
we fought over a toy. I pushed Jeeter,
and he would fall to the ground, then get up

and knock me to the ground. I would get up,
and the match continued, until his father,
who had a belly full of *Pabst,* ordered
his son to hit me with a piece of brick.
Jeeter obeyed his father for once.
Fortunately, God blessed me with a hard head.
But when my father heard how Mr. Jones
bragged to neighbors about his son's exploits,
he went down bent on bloodying Jeeter's dad.
Bang! Bang! Bang! Dad rapped on Mr. Jones' door.
But like a boxer not answering the bell,
his rattling door was left unanswered. And, so,
no paddy wagon would need dispatching,
as my father's wrath finally subsided.

"Hey Matt, what happened to your face?" Jeeter asked,
while bounce passing a basketball my way.
"Chasing fly balls again, were you?" He needled.
"Still better lookin' than your mug," I said,
while swishing a jump shot from 20 feet.
"Yeah, I suppose that's why I'm with a hottie,
and you're with that skank named *nobody.*
"Shut up and give me the ball, moron," I said.
"Gotta match for this joint?" Jeeter asked.
I struck a flame and drew hard on the joint;
its buzz was direct and got right to the point.
Weed had become an herb in my garden.
My heart had already started to harden.

*   *   *

Part Five, Buzz Kill

Too bad my brain has a mind of its own!
Why did I let myself talk me into
installing this stereo system
in my *Mustang?* I didn't know what
I was doing. But did that stop me?
No, of course not. So nothing but static now!
"We're in the home half of the second inning,"
Chuck Thompson's voice cracks from the radio,
"with the O's leading the A's 1-0.
Tony Armas takes Palmer's pitch for strike one."
As water in my bong starts bubbling again,
whispers from *Budweiser* and weed entice me:
Drive! You can still do it. You'll be okay.
"Armas lines one! Snagged by Belanger at short,
who dove headlong to his left," Thompson exclaims,
interrupting my temptation for now.

"What's up, Willy? Outta weed again?" I ask.
"It's been dry, man. Do you have any, Matt?"
"Were ya not just engulfed in a cloud of it,
when ya opened my car door? Have a seat,
but don't sit your fat butt on my *Doritos*."
Willy Austin is an acquaintance, someone
I've tolerated but never really liked.
He's much more intelligent than he lets on
and likes to hit on other guys' girlfriends.
I don't mind sharing some weed with Willy,
but only every once in a while, though.

"Palmer misses with his fastball, walking
Cliff Johnson with two outs in the second.
That brings catcher Rick Dempsey to the mound
to chat with Palmer," Thompson tells us.
"Baseball's boring. I don't like it," Willy says,
while some of my pot and one of my smokes
are disappearing into his lungs.
"When are you going to smoke *Marlboros*, Matt?
I can't stomach these nasty menthols of yours."
"You've been bummin' cigarettes from me
for seven years. Don't ya know by now,
I only smoke *Salems* to tick your dumb,
redneck butt off? Ya moronic mooch!"
Pointing my middle finger at him, I say,
"Now, here's your map to the *Marlboro* store.
Ya got a lotta nerve, Willy. No,
ya can't have one of my beers. Besides,
aren't ya a *Miller* man, anyway?"
"No, Matt. I like *Budweiser*. You know that."
"Then grab me one too, ya jerk," I say.
"No! I'm not turning on 98 Rock!
And shut up about it already, will ya?
I don't even remember invitin' ya
over here to listen to the game with me,
buzz kill! What's up with ya anyway?"
"Sell me a joint's worth of weed, Matt. Come on."
"I don't sell marijuana to narcs, ya fool."
"I'm not a narcotics officer, Matt.
You know that. I don't want people to think that."
"Hey, Willy, it's a joke. Lighten up!

19

And don't let the door hit ya in the rear end
on your way out. No! Ya can't have another
one of my *Budweisers* for the road."
Willy could have taken one of my Buds,
and, of course, I'd never have been the wiser—
and the pun is certainly intended!
But since he's in the dark about my blindness,
he doesn't know how my lack of sight offers
much more speed to his hand, when considering
this adage: *The hand is quicker than the eye!*
I cling to secrecy for protection,
but for how long will my armament shield me?
Or is it a delusion, and, perhaps,
already as clear as a cloudless sky
to the outside world? Is the joke on me?
Since my albatross has been defined today,
I can reveal it and explain it. Right?
Wrong! It's something I've held onto for too long.
Something I've earned. Something I've nurtured.
No one can have it. It's mine, at least for now.

*   *   *

Part Six, Sold Out

Just a few weeks after ninth grade started
at my new school, in Brooklyn, Maryland,
called Benjamin Franklin Junior High,
a crookedly placed decal that said *SOLD*
partially covered *FOR SALE* on the sign
in my front yard. The smile smeared on the face of
that woman glued to it seemed to have widened
in contrast to the frown that restricted mine.
Pasadena would soon be my new home.
Since drug use and the crime rate was rising,
faster than Tropical Storm Agnes had raised
her flood waters in 1972,
mom and dad, both filled with best intentions,
decided to throw my sister and me
in a *U-Haul* and drive us away, before
the raging current reached our front door. Too late!

I don't remember much about what I learned
in reading, writing, or arithmetic class.
Education consisted mostly of how
to shoulder myself through the idiocy
of racial tension, that seethed—like a pot
of grand mom's bubbling crab soup—through the halls
that snaked through Benjamin Franklin Junior High.
After entering school, on one sunny day,
I paused in the hallway to allow my eyes
a moment to recover from *timeout*,
while inadvertently impeding progress

of several schoolmates of mine. One of whom
literally kicked me in my butt
and ordered, *gitcha white a** out the way.*
Assailed by a din of Babel and darkness,
the hall constricted me like a boa,
so I kept my mouth shut and knife pocketed.
Sightless, it was useless as a drinking straw.
It was more of a security blanket
than a security measure. Anyway,
what I took away from class that day was this:
ignorance was a double-edged sword
that cuts both ways in regard to race.

That afternoon, my newspapers arrived late;
and after my sister volunteered to help
with them, mom only further delayed us:
"Matt, Cindy, come on," she yelled through our yard
for my sister and me to come in and get
ready for dinner. "Wait a minute, mom.
We still have piles of papers to fold," I said.
"They can wait till after dinner," mom countered.
"The food's gonna get cold and dad's hungry."
By then, I'd delivered papers two years
for *The News American.* Dad and I
connected somehow through my paper route,
since he also had one when he was a boy.
One fond memory I have was waking up
early on Sunday mornings to deliver
newspapers with my father. After stacking
my papers into an old wooden wagon,

and with our sweaty arms stained with their ink,
we pulled it along on its squeaky wheels,
which cried out in thirst for a sip of oil.
Some papers plopped on customers' doorsteps,
others slid to a stop at their *Welcome* mats.
And after the last paper plunked on its porch,
mom rewarded us with plates piled with pancakes.

"Go to war, Jack," mom hollered at my father,
sounding like the voice of Edith Bunker.
"You're not havin' chocolate puddin' for dinner
again. Are ya? I got Irish Stew, ya know!"
This mixture of onions, spam, and potatoes
topped off our empty stomachs on many nights.
Mom tossed out her catchphrase, *Go to war, Jack,*
every time my dad did something that riled her.
I never learned the meaning of the term,
but I laughed, if not outwardly, then at least
inwardly, each time she would burst out with it.
"Ya want some more Irish Stew, Matt?" Mom asked,
while flitting about like a gnat, already
clearing the soiled dishes from the table.
"Sure, mom," I said, "I'm still starvin'. Pile it on!"
"We'll be movin' into our new house
on November 30," dad heralded
candidly between bites of buttered bread
and spoonfuls of piping hot chocolate pudding.
While my freshly filled plate of stew sat untouched,
I calculated the days remaining till
11/30/74.

The next day, I argued with my dad and said,
"I've already seen the place enough times.
I don't need to go again. We just went there
last weekend. I remember what it looks like!
I wanna play basketball here today.
And besides, we'll be livin' there soon enough.
I wanna enjoy the time I still have here."
"Ya can play basketball later. Come on.
Let's go!" Dad commanded. On the way
to tour our new house and neighborhood again,
the cancer of contempt spread through my smirk,
and no amount of chemo could cure it,
as the portrait of Lakeland faded
through the back window of my father's Ford.

Our new house was a split-foyer, single home.
It sat on a small peninsula
about one-quarter mile from Grays Creek,
which was like a tongue that projected
from the mouth of the Magothy River
and licked the edge of our community.
Space crowded around our new house, instead of
other homes like how it was in Lakeland.
Thick woods stood out back, where an alley should run.
It was much too quiet and way too slow.
But this was where mom and dad had awakened
from their *American Dream*. For years,
they sweated many hours laboring,
and so each of them deserved this higher rung
on the socio-economic ladder.

And although the perch wasn't *that* high up,
it was still high enough for my nose to bleed.

Only if clouds would rain some gas on this place,
and a lightning bolt would strike it like a match!
As my daydream stoked this inferno,
I pondered the path my footsteps treaded on,
while walking down my new street to the beach.
Time to get used to this fork my life's taken
onto Maryland Avenue, where
my new home was burning in my mind.
I dragged my feet on passed the baseball diamond,
vowing to myself never to play on it—
and not to voice how foul I was afield.
Crap! I cursed, when I clipped my kneecap
on a thin cable, barely visible,
threading its way through scores of pilings,
stationed around the borders of the beach.
I stepped on the pier and sat down on the dock,
dangling my feet just a foot above Grays Creek.
I fired up a *Salem* and took a deep drag;
the smoke mingled with salt air and creosote,
a pleasant scent in an odd sort of way.
Echoes throbbed in the air from a basketball,
bouncing from somewhere off in the distance.
Around the pier, it was like inside
a bionic ear, where sounds were magnified
in the vast openness of the creek.
The volume from the once faint voices of
the basketball players suddenly increased

into what sounded like a screaming match.
A touch of Lakeland at last, I laughed,
while watching my *Salem* drown in Grays Creek.
"Time to go, Matt." Dad hollered from his Ford.
"We got a lotta packin' to do. Come on!"

*   *   *

Part Seven, Stairway to Heaven

My *Mustang* and I have this in common:
our luster continues to tarnish,
like a corpse rotting in a casket!
As a mental mist clouds my memories,
my musing shifts back to present tense, where
RP cells have latched onto each retina,
like a herd of ants ravaging a *Cheez-It,*
that some careless hand let slip to the floor.
Dang if it ain't like I've spent twenty-one years
working out without having weights on the bar!
I can't even say, *The world's passing me by,*
as I sit, bound to this seat, watching the world
stand still through my *Mustang's* sap-stained windshield,
while distortion overwhelms my perception.
As plume after plume of pot smoke wraps me
in its cancerous haze, the wind breathlessly
moans like a dying man's cries for his momma.

"A's 2, O's 1, with Al Bumbry batting
in the top of the third inning," Thompson says.
"Langford's curveball's low and away. Ball one."
Still staving off sobriety for now,
a glow shimmers from the belly of my bowl,
then fizzles out like fireworks on the Fourth,
as the smoke paws at my lungs like a bull
about to maul a clown at a rodeo.
I mute the game and slip Zeppelin in its sheath,
after the 8-track winds and jerks, out pours:

There's a lady who's sure all that glitters is gold
And she's buying a stairway to heaven.

Cranking up "Stairway to Heaven," I ponder
the surreal ride to work I had yesterday,
when that foul breath, that belched from Curtis Bay's
industrial throats, pressed upon us, while dad
drove me to my job at the machine shop.
But while en route, my mind began to snore,
as dad sat behind the steering wheel
of his pulpit, preaching about God,
the Gospel, and some Book in the Bible
he referred to as Revelation.
Above the snores that thundered inside my head,
these lyrics from Rush the rock group whined,
My mind is not for rent to any god or government.
Dad, meanwhile, spun on, like a Michelin
down Curtis Avenue, explaining how
in the future seven years of Great
Tribulation would plague our planet, God
pouring out judgment from His cup of wrath
on populations, who, at that time,
will have turned away from Him to follow
Satan, his False Prophet, and Beast. What on earth
was dad talking about? I wondered
in the machine shop at lunchtime yesterday,
as I rested on my splintered workbench,
tired already from a morning of tasting
asbestos shavings from gasket making.
On the filter of my *Salem*, I smoked

and swilled some *Coke*, contemplating Christ,
clueless of His Second Coming, Salvation,
or any Great Tribulation—but my own.
Yet I heard Scripture whispering to me!

Ooh, it makes me wonder;
Ooh, it makes me wonder.

And though I'm not ready to open that Book,
the way I think about it and Christ has changed.
It intrigues me now how the Bible speaks
of the Second Coming of Jesus Christ—and
other future events it says will happen.
Dad told me, and not for the first time,
that Jesus loved me so much so that He died
on the cross to forgive me of my sins.
I felt the love of Jesus yesterday
for the first time. He has my attention.
Dad said that if I repented from my sin—
agreed with God that I sinned against Him—
and believed that Jesus died on the cross
for my sins, and that God His Father
raised Him from the dead, He would save me
from hell and give me eternal life.
All I had to do was call on His name.
I'm not ready for that commitment yet,
but I know I'm a sinner, that's obvious!

Yes, there are two paths you can go by, but in the long run
There's still time to change the road you're on

Ooh, it makes me wonder
Ooh, Ooh, it makes me wonder

But mom raised me Catholic, took me to church.
I'm a born and bred Catholic boy, baptized
with holy water, made my first communion,
went to confession, and was confirmed—
an altar boy with eight years of Catholic school!
Yet emptiness overflows inside my soul.
Is it because Catholic boys need Jesus, too?
Religion never was important to dad.
That is until we relocated here—
to the suburbs in Pasadena—and he
started attending a church up the street:
Lake Shore Baptist. I've gone a few times.
Now, he's a freakin' deacon, of all things.
That's when he started telling not only me
but even all our neighbors about Jesus,
and only God knows who else. Embarrassing!
Couldn't he have taken up golf instead?

Your head is humming and it won't go,
in case you don't know
The piper's calling you to join him

Why do *I* have to face blindness, God?
I know life ain't fair. But this *really* ain't fair!
I wanna see a baseball hit from a bat,
and find a woman who will love me,
and not discard me because of my blindness;

30

I wanna drive and find a career;
I want sight to reel me in from the margins
of both society and darkness.
I don't wanna feel shame from not seeing,
for being misunderstood for my blind-
induced follies that trip me up daily.
Intoxication is like dark glasses,
that I hide behind to cover my blindness.
It's easier to blame insobriety
for my stupid stunts than for me to admit
that most of the blame belongs to this phantom
that clings to me every day and every night,
an obstacle builder blighting my path.
He can't hurt me here inside my armor,
where I wield cans of *Budweiser* and weed.

And if you listen very hard
The tune will come to you at last
When all is one and one is all, yeah
To be a rock and not to roll.

And she's buying the stairway to heaven . . . .

*   *   *

Part Eight, The Move

Our time to depart from Lakeland arrived:
it was 11/30/74.
And although the location of my life
on that Saturday was about to change,
other parts of it would remain the same:
"How many times have I told ya, Matt,
'do NOT smoke in this house?'" Mom scolded.
"Uncle Sherman does," I argued. "And besides,
it's our last day here. So what's the difference?"
Stationed with an air of impatience,
the *U-Haul* sat idling on our street, until
dad thwarted its flow of fuel with the turn
of a key. He and Uncle Sherman,
who volunteered to help us move, opened
the container door and pulled its ramp out
onto the ground: a 45 degree plank
to transport all our possessions on.
"Go to war, Jack, be careful with my hutch.
Ya guys almost hit the top of the doorway!"
Mom squawked, supervising from the sidewalk.
"So, Mare, ya wanna do it?" Dad retorted.

Lakeland was like a loved one to me,
who was about to die, with a physician
prepared to pull the plug on its life support.
And just like how, when a person passed away,
people never refrained from going about
their daily business, as if nothing happened,

so, too, the neighborhood continued
to rotate anesthetized on its axis—
the normal order of a Saturday
interrupted only by our *U-Haul,*
anchored in its harbor on Norland Road.
That ship, with its container stuffed with cargo,
had already departed three times
for Pasadena and had returned again—
this time to reload for its final voyage.

"I'm goin' for a bike ride, dad, I'll be back."
"Don't be long, Matt. I wanna be gone by dark."
I bicycled against a breeze that slapped
at my chilled face. A few degrees colder,
my tears would have frosted on my cheeks.
I parked my bike at the top of the hill,
overlooking the park I played at for years.
After five matches I finally breathed life
into my *Salem,* while it stole mine. Even
while dusk slowly began to rob the sky
of its day, light still ruled from lofty lamps
that hovered high above our city streets.
Still not a soul around, it was as if
only ghosts had come out for play: not a peep
except from seats of swings smacking each other,
and the clanging from their twisting chains,
both elbowed about by the whirling wind.
More action in the 'burbs of Pasadena
than in my beloved Lakeland tonight,
I mused, while, at the same time, studying

that ever-present ball glove, which drooped sadly
from the middle of my handlebars.
Since my life had become permanently like
that season between the World Series
and Spring Training, what use would I have
anymore for some moth-eaten ball glove?
Slinging it like a *Frisbee*, I watched as it
cartwheeled to a stop, out of season, and so,
there, I left it upon that brittle hill.
And after I drove to my house one last time,
I pedaled up the plank of the *U-Haul*
and parked my bike in the back of the truck.
While my dad shut the door, I took one last look
around my street, branding it onto my mind,
then watched my sister climb into the cab,
dragging her *Mrs. Beasley* doll, wrapped
in a bedraggled blanket, behind her.

By the time we unpacked our *U-Haul*,
nighttime deepened in Pasadena.
Raindrops, meanwhile, started to pelt us,
like birdshot being tossed from the heavens.
Hurrying to the house, I clipped my hand
on the corner of a column that pillared
an awning on the face of our house.
I staggered, dazed in the darkness, dropping
the box I carried. After squeezing my hand,
and, then, performing the *ouch-ouch-ouch* dance,
I put my hand in front of my face and saw
nothing! Was I the only one who noticed

this darkness in Pasadena, Maryland?
If not, no one else certainly mentioned it.
"Take your shoes off before ya come in here,"
mom commanded, as I walked through the front door.

As I settled into my bed that night,
the smell of fresh lumber reminded me
of Mr. Smith's woodshop class at my old school.
And, then, I thought about how the *woods*
we used to romp through in our old yard, back
in Lakeland, had consisted of just three trees:
a plum, a maple, and a crabapple.
Each of which dwarfed in comparison to
the scores of oaks that towered in our new yard.
They danced that night to the music of a storm,
which played like a band engaged in a concert
in the nearby bay, while sharp winds sawed off
the limbs that bombarded our roof. I worried
not about the storm but about beginning
a new school in the middle of the year.
On Monday, my terror would begin,
as a new student at George Fox Junior High.
And who the heck was George Fox, anyway?
Before the track of my thinking dissolved
into sleep, apprehension had begun
its strategy to shear away my courage,
like a shepherd fleecing sheep from his flock.

I wanted this day to be put to bed
months before it arrived, but, since our school day

began at noon, by the time I started
down the street to catch the bus at its stop,
Monday morning had already dragged on,
like a midnight mass on Christmas Eve.
If only I had some pot to caulk the seams
of my nerves. Instead, to grapple with panic,
I chain-smoked seven straight cigarettes.
Meanwhile, as I lumbered toward the bus stop,
as if my feet had been manacled,
a guy approached me in a jean jacket
with a bandana, that, perhaps, might have been
tied a little too tight around his head.
"Hey, you moved into that new house up the street.
Didn't you?" "Yep." I said. "Yeah, I saw you
Saturday in your yard. Yeah, we were hoping
that, since your family room now sits on
one of our favorite partying trails,
some pretty girls might move in to compensate
for our loss. Disappointed again, I see!
You're Matt, right?" "Yeah," I said. "How did ya know that?"
"I have to get my *Of Mice and Men* book.
Ninth grade has to write a paper on it.
Hey, do you have an extra cigarette?"
I tossed him a *Salem*. "What's this? Menthol?
It'll do, until I get some *Marlboros*.
I'm Nathan Carlyle, by the way. See ya!"
You're welcome, moron. I thought to myself.
And ya never did answer my question!

Beyond the normal fears I fretted about

starting a new school at the midyear mark,
like making new friends, fitting in, and over-
coming the new-kid-on-the-block stigma,
anxiousness over what visual mishaps
that might await me became a pestilence,
circulating through the veins of my mind.
I kept telling myself over and over,
Just pay attention and you'll be all right.
Since seeing had become such a chore, though,
just paying attention might not be
a powerful enough lens for clarity.
Whatever ya do, I reminded myself,
don't sit on anyone when ya get on
that bus and your eyes go into timeout mode,
like that time, on the 28 Lakeland Bus,
when ya unwittingly sat on the lap
of that elderly woman. And the guy
next to her, probably misinterpreting
your blunder as disrespect, hollered:
"What the heck's wrong with you, jerk? Didn't you
see her sitting there? Open your eyes next time!"
I felt like I was back in right field again,
with the bases loaded, praying my old prayer:
Please don't let 'em hit the ball my way!

As the noon hour grew ever closer,
I jumped into the bus stop with both feet,
like a swimmer who plunges into a pool
to get acclimated to the cold water.
A girl with dark, ratty hair balanced her butt

quite delicately on a cable festooned
between two pilings, both hands on a book
that absorbed her face. "Whaddya readin'?"
"Steinbeck's *Of Mice and Men*," she said, her eyes
still screwed to the pages. "Who are you?" She asked.
"I'm Matt Harris, just moved in up the street."
"I'm Liz Knowles," she said, unfastening
her eyes from her book. "Your first day, huh?"
"Yep," I said. "That must suck! Gotta smoke?" She asked.
Does anyone here have their own cigarettes?
I wondered to myself, promising to stop
being the neighborhood cigarette machine.
After lighting a *Salem* for her,
she gave her attention back to Steinbeck.

The bus grumbled to a halt. And I followed
Liz up its steps, on passed the driver,
while my eyes went into *timeout* mode.
But since the bus wasn't too crowded,
I landed safely in an empty seat.
So far, so good. Just pay attention, Matt,
I reminded myself, as my eyes focused.
Liz lounged in the last seat of the bus, knees pressed
against the seat in front of her, head back
staring intently at the ceiling.
As the bus filled, while making its rounds,
I felt invisible, as more kids poured on,
yet was grateful no one sat beside me.

The noontime sun reflected from the concrete,

and pierced through my eyes like a sewing needle,
stitching a tapestry of blinding light,
through which I maneuvered from the bus
to the entrance of George Fox Junior High School.
As I fell in with a flow of kids, despite
my internal admonition to myself—

Pay attention. Don't run into anyone—

I still stepped on and bumped into people, while
excuse me seemed like the only words I knew.
On the one hand, I felt as if I stood out,
like a lone tree surrounded by a vast field.
While at the same time, on the other hand,
I felt as if I were dead, like a ghost
that floated through the land of the living.

At last, I found *English 147.*
As I walked through the door, the bell sounded.
"Hi, I'm Matt Harris. This is my first day,"
I said to my first period teacher.
"Let me see. Yes. There you are in my roll book,"
she said. "Nice to meet you. My name is
Mrs. Czyrwiezki. But call me Mrs. C.
Oh, here, take this book, *Of Mice and Men,*
by John Steinbeck. The class is reading it.
Are you familiar with the book, Matt?"
"No ma'am," I said, "But I have seen the movie."
"Great," Mrs. C said, "You take a seat,
right over there behind Gregory Kilmer.

He's that gentleman in the green jacket."
Green was as foreign as Greek to me;
but worse than that, Mrs. C must have pointed
to where Gregory Kilmer was seated.
And, of course, my peripheral vision
did not detect her simple directions,
so I wandered off in the opposite way,
where that familiar sound—laughter—greeted me.
"You stoned or something, dude? Greg's over there,"
one of my classmates said, my central vision
picking up his finger pointing to where
that gentleman in the green jacket sat.
I slunk off to my desk and opened Steinbeck,
wishing to hide myself inside its pages.

After the final bell rang at 5:30,
everyone flew through the doors in a frenzy.
Darkness had already descended
on the parking lot packed with buses and kids.
And though *whiteout,* at least, left my eyes alone,
blackness slowed my pace more than a little bit,
as I looked from the sidewalk, where I trudged.
While searching for bus number *249,*
impact to my shins suddenly startled me.
It was like a soccer striker had struck them,
while attempting to steal the ball from me.
I tossed my binder like a hot potato
and braced myself with both hands to brake my fall,
as pain pounded from my ankles to my knees.
That familiar foe—laughter—blasted at me,

while kids walked by without any hands to help.
I stooped and felt along the ground to find
the place where my loose-leaf binder landed.
Later, I realized I had tripped into
a large box filled with frozen earth, designed
not for an idiot like me to fall in
but for a large flower garden to bloom in.
"Over here, Matt. Liz yelled from the bus,"
apparently having witnessed my mishap.
And as if nothing had happened, I embarked
on *249* for the long ride home.

When we arrived at our stop, *whiteout,*
timeout, and poor peripheral vision
at that hour had become nonissues, since
darkness had trumped the trio. I saw nothing
but shades of light that flickered from porch lamps.
I walked home with my left foot on the shoulder,
and my right foot on the road, wondering how
I would find my house, until I caught
a glimpse of dad's *Galaxie* in our driveway,
painted with light that was brushed by the beams
illuminating from the lamp in our yard.
I felt for my keys and opened the door,
engulfed by Irish Stew's homespun smell,
its spices mingling with mom's command:
"Go to war, Matt, take your shoes off, will ya?"

*   *   *

Part Nine, Old Grand-Dad

Yanking Zeppelin from its 8-track chamber,
I bash the dash again, tuning in the game,
as Eddie Murray rounds the bases, after
belting a solo blast to tie the score
at 2 in the top of the fourth inning.
I should probably sell my *Mustang* before
it falls apart and won't be worth a dime bag.
"Claws, what the heck ya sneakin' up on me for?
Ya scared the crap right out of me, man."
"I'm not sneakin'. I'm just peekin' at this rust
that's eatin' away at your quarter panel,"
Claws says, while sipping some *Old Grand-Dad*.
"When ya puttin' her back on the road, Matt?"
"When I get the money, I guess," I lied.
"Ya already work fulltime, dude. Ya need
to find a new job makin' more money,
before this beauty wastes away for good."
Claws' real name is Brian Crabtree,
but everybody always calls him Claws.
He likes whiskey, particularly *Old Grand-Dad*.
That habit began in tenth grade, after
a flame felled a local store called *Angels*.
When the ashes and brimstone settled, Claws
and I paid a visit to dear *Old Grand-Dad*,
salvaging cases from fallen *Angels*.
We hauled in our arms a load of spirits
across the parking lot, where Claws spotted
a cop in his squad car on patrol—

probably on the lookout for looters!
We took cover inside a patch of tall weeds,
where the cop's light seemed incomprehensible
to the darkness that it barely dented.
Not breathing a breath until the law left,
Claws and I were drunk on adrenalin,
and for months afterward drunk on *Old Grand-Dad*.
By then, I had learned to maneuver quite well
at night by listening to my friends' footsteps
and following the sounds of their movements.
And though I memorized the trails we passed through,
many times I still would walk into trees,
or trip on an unanticipated bump.
"Who's winnin'?" Claws asks. "It's tied at 2," I say.
"Wanna go see who's hangin' out down The Park?"
"Nah. Maybe I'll catch up with ya later.
I'm gonna finish listenin' to the game."
Claws always perceived something was amiss
with my sight, but I always changed the subject
whenever that troublesome issue arose.
One time he advised that I should look down
more often when I walked at nighttime.
He wasn't being a smart aleck, though.
He was really trying to help me out.

"John Lowenstein fouls off Mark Langford's fastball.
And the count is even: one ball, one strike,"
Chuck Thompson says, calling the game from his booth.
"Lowenstein's batting two forty-nine this year
and struck out in his first at bat today.

Langford throws a low outside breaking ball,
and Lowenstein hits a slow roller
toward second baseman, Shooty Babitt,
who tosses it over to Jim Spencer
at first for the final out of the inning,"
Thompson bellows, before sending us off
to listen to more stupid commercials,
putting me asleep for awhile until . . .

"Hey, Matt, wake up. Ya alright?" Jenny Young asks,
her fist banging on my driver's-side roof.
"Yeah. I just nodded off a bit. What's up?"
"I'm gettin' some stuff for mom at the store.
Ya wanna walk up with me?" She asks.
"Nah. I just wanna stay here and catch a buzz."
"Looks like you're already buzzed. Somethin' wrong?"
"Just thinkin' about some things, that's all."
"It looked like ya wuz snoozin' more than thinkin',"
Jenny chuckles, then reminiscing, says,
"Hey! Remember when *you* used to shop for mom?
She'd give ya a store list. You'd steal the crap
and only charge her half price for the stuff.
Mom always loves gettin' a good bargain."
"Yeah, of course, I remember. I'm not senile."
"Keep smokin' that wacky weed and ya will be."
"Ya smoke it way more than I do, girl."
"Yeah, but I have more brain cells to burn than you."
Jenny needles, while heading off to the store.
"Hey. Bring me back some *Doritos*," I yell.
Jenny and I have been close friends for years;

and though I'm clueless about her eye color,
I still love the way they flicker when she laughs.
And all of us guys around here agree:
she fills out her *Levis* rather nicely.
But what I like best about her is this:
we can talk effortlessly for hours.
And, yet, as easily as we converse,
I still can't share with her my ordeal.

*　　*　　*

Part Ten, Angel Dust

During the first few months at my new school,
ninth grade moved along at a pace not unlike
how a lazy man might prepare for work.
While the feet of winter trudged through its season,
even in February, I liked our beach.
When the creek lapped away at the shoreline
on a windy day, it sprayed my soul with peace.
The locals referred to the beach as *The Park*;
and since now I was a bona fide *local*,
I began to call the beach The Park, too.
I had met a few people by then, but still
felt all alone as if I didn't exist.
Liz Knowles introduced me to Ralphie Nelson,
our neighborhood drug dealer. Ralphie
drove a light-colored Toyota *Corolla*,
didn't work, didn't go to school, just sold drugs.
Whenever his *Corolla* cruised by The Park,
it conjured up in my mind the snowball truck
that once rumbled through the streets of Lakeland.
In contrast to that little kid I once was,
who thirsted for a strawberry snowball,
with a mountain of marshmallow on top,
I hungered now with other teenagers
for a nickel or a dime bag of weed,
or a hearty hunk of black or blonde hashish.
And unlike how we once had to yell to halt
the snowball truck, as we chased it down the street,
who at times had even forgotten to brake,

we never once hollered *wait a minute*
for Ralphie. He always stopped when he saw us,
to earn his ill-gotten gain by feeding
his patrons' chemical dependencies,
while exploiting that abyss which existed
in each and every one of our lost souls.

Darkness was just about to cast its net,
as I approached the driver's-side window.
"What goodies ya got today, Ralphie?" I asked.
"Ya seen Nathan?" Ralphie asked. "No." I said.
"Let's ride. We're wasting heat." Ralphie said,
turning up "Smoke on the Water" full throttle.
As soon as I shut the passenger's-side door,
he lit a joint, inhaled, and passed it my way.
Exhaling into a creaking cough,
he snorted and shouted, "Red Mexican!"
His hacking betrayed the harshness of his weed.
Still, I took a hit, but not too deeply,
and passed it back to him, "A bit coarse," I said.
His throaty laugh clashed with his sales pitch: "After
a few hits it'll taste as smooth as
a *Marlboro*." "This crap will turn your lungs
inside out," I said. After another hit,
I passed it back, hoping to finish
the darn thing before nightfall. It was always
troublesome for me to see a joint or bowl,
when someone handed it to me in the dark.
Even though I focused on the fiery glow,
sometimes I would still lose sight of it,

whenever something distracted me, or
whenever it fizzled out; usually,
when I missed it, I just blamed it on the buzz.
Yet it created angst for me, and I'm sure
question marks arose in the minds of my friends.
Not to mention when I partied with Ralphie,
I always feared we'd get busted, as he drove
and sold drugs throughout our neighborhood.

"Grab that *roach clip* in the glove box," Ralphie said.
"We can get a couple more hits from this."
About a quarter inch of the joint remained;
at that length, it was referred to as a roach.
Roach clips were like tweezers that hooked on it,
useful tools that kept your fingers away
from the heat while you held it. But most
importantly no weed would get wasted—
only the people who were smoking it!
When we stopped back at The Park, he snatched
Deep Purple from out of the 8-track player,
as I pulled ten bucks from my wallet and bought
a dime bag of Ralphie's *Red Mexican.*
My sense of touch told me it was a good count;
and my sense of smell told me it was pot;
and that was really all I needed to know.
Before I could put the baggie away,
someone banged on my window and yelled, "Busted!"
"Nathan, ya must have mush for brains," Ralphie roared,
as I rolled down my window and saw blackness.
"I ought to whoop up on ya," he added.

"Open up, burnout! It's cold," Nathan ordered,
before squeezing into the backseat.

Nathan Carlyle went to the same church my mom
took my sister and me to: St. Jane Francis—
another *fine* Catholic boy just like me.
But our similarities ended there.
He seemed to conceal a Judas-like spirit,
which betrayed him; for whenever people left
from a party, he would, more often than not,
shoot arrows of insults at their backs.
I wondered if it had ever occurred
to those, who had laughed along with Nathan, that,
after they would leave, he targeted them, too.

"I finally found some flakes for you, Ralphie,"
Nathan bragged, while loading up a bowl.
"It took ya long enough," Ralphie chided.
"Oh! And, by the way, moron, I didn't mean
Frosted Flakes," Ralphie teased. "And I hope
Tony the Tiger didn't bite ya,"
I added, as Ralphie roared: *"They're Grrrrreat!"*
Nathan smacked me hard in the head. Instantly,
I turned toward the darkness and warned,
"Touch me again, Nathan, and I'll bash ya."
"If you're gonna whoop up on him, Matt, just don't
bloody my car," Ralphie chuckled. "I gotta
go find me a tree to water," he said.
After Ralphie bolted through the door,
Nathan said to me, "I wish he'd take a bath

sometimes. He always smells like a litter box.
You know what I mean, Matt?" "Not really," I lied.

Flakes were parsley treated with a drug
called Phencyclidine or PCP,
also known on the street as *Angel Dust*.
This dust, however, did not descend from
any angelic host from heaven, though;
but rather it ascended from fallen ones,
imprisoned in the chambers of Hades.
But regardless of its origins, it was
a hallucinogenic that rocketed
my friends and me to other universes!
After Ralphie had returned from his mission,
the flake bowl made its rounds throughout the night
in a triangular fashion: from Nathan,
sitting in the middle of the backseat,
to Ralphie, stationed behind the wheel,
then to me, in the front passenger's-side seat.
When a sizzling sound started inside my ears,
like bacon frying in a skillet,
I knew this crackling was internal, because
Ralphie blasted Black Sabbath full volume,
blocking out all noise but Ozzy Osbourne.
Were these lost souls hissing in hell? I wondered,
while a shudder seized me. I was mesmerized
by what seemed like a demon shoveling
a grave with a corrupt spade in the basement
of my psyche. I saw an iron gate,
though not upright, but lying on the ground,

and not a single pearl decorated it!
Night swallowed me up in Ralphie's *Corolla*,
blinding my physical eyes completely.
Yet clearly I saw this horror flick
projected on the screen of my mind.
Was that Cerberus' bark, that hellish hound,
with his three heads, guarding Hades' door?

My turn came to draw from the pipe again,
while watching the parsley flakes twinkle like stars.
Ralphie started up the *Corolla* and yelled,
"Let it ride," as his tires squealed, while fishtailing
on the frigid, February road.
It was as if we had become detached,
like little children participating
in parallel play, each of us engaged
in our own unique hallucination,
with the bowl of flakes as our primary toy.
Ralphie's driving seemed so precise, as if
the car glided along like a monorail.
The lights from oncoming traffic appeared
as if they were about to jump in our lane,
and we wouldn't have felt the pain if they had.
We were on a magic carpet ride, indeed!
Every time the last flake flickered out,
Nathan topped off the bowl with another batch,
like an attentive barkeep filling a glass
with spirits as soon as someone emptied it.
The more I smoked the more I sank into
a dimension beyond the physical realm,

conjuring up influences from domains
that breached my borders and trespassed through my soul.
When Ralphie stopped back at The Park again,
I opened the car, wordless, and stepped out
into the cold air that warmed me with relief.
My feet felt bare through my *Easy Walker* shoes,
thinking for some reason they'd been sliced open.
As I touched them, they were perfectly intact,
while numbness permeated my body,
not from cold but from some foreign entity.
As I wandered home from The Park, I treaded
gingerly on the double-yellow lines,
when I spotted them from collateral light,
amid the barren road that led back home.
And like how poets use lines in their poems
to pilot their craft toward epiphany,
the double-yellows likewise captained me
through the haze to the unveiling of my house.
While fear that the street might sever my feet
slashed through my thinking like a razorblade,
I hallucinated that I had fallen
straight down through the earth, until my chin
landed between the double-yellows,
while inching onward toward my goal,
as that ceaseless sound of bacon sizzled,
its hellish grease splattering inside my head,
until I entered my deserted house,
then dreamt while wide awake until the dawn.

"Matt, it's noon. Ya gonna sleep all day?" Mom yelled,

striking the side of my bed with her broom.
"Go help dad with the paneling in his den."
It was like I'd awakened from delusion
and still was unable to discern the parts
that were fact from the ones which were fiction.
While confusion daunted my demeanor,
the smell of bacon drove me to the kitchen.
Its sizzle jerked me back again to last night.
"Hey Face," I greeted my sister, as she flipped
bacon that bathed in a pool of grease.
"Shut up! Mom, Matt's calling me names again."
For no reason, other than to torment her,
I often referred to my sister as Face.
She hated when I dragged the "f" sound out:
"Fa-Fa-Fa-Face stop you're tattlin'," I taunted.
"Leave your sister alone," mom bellowed
from her bedroom down at the end of the hall.
"Bye Fa-Fa-Fa-Face" I teased again, swiping
some slices of bacon that cooled on a plate.

"How's the den comin' along, dad?" I asked.
"I gotta go to the hardware store for nails.
Do ya wanna ride up there with me?"
"Sure. I need to buy some smokes, anyway."
While getting into my dad's Ford *Galaxie*,
I heard Ralphie and his dad, Ralph, Sr.,
start to laugh, while standing in their front yard,
neither having responded to my wave.
That's odd, I thought, as dad sped away.
"I invited Mr. Ralph to church," dad said.

Oh great, I thought, *that probably explains why
they were laughing and had ignored me.*
A couple of weeks after we had moved here,
dad started attending Lake Shore Baptist Church,
right up the street about a mile from our house.
Dad changed soon after he first sat on their pew,
from a man who rarely ever spoke of God
to a man who could not shut up about Him.
"So what did Mr. Ralph tell ya?" I asked.
"He said he didn't believe in fairytales,"
dad answered, in a lamentable tone.
*Dang! Ain't it hard enough for me to fit in
around here*, I thought, *without my father
tellin' the whole neighborhood about Jesus?*

"For God so loved the world, Matt, that he gave his
only begotten Son, that whosoever
believeth in him should not perish,
but have everlasting life" (John 3:16),
dad said. "God doesn't want anyone in hell,
tormented by its flame forever.
But it's your sin and mine that put us there.
That's why He sent Jesus, His Son, to die
on the cross to forgive us of our sins.
It's God's gift to us, the greatest gift ever.
And all we have to do is receive it,
by grace through faith, by repenting from our sin,
and by believing in the Lord Jesus Christ."
Dad finished his piece, as we pulled into
the local hardware store called Aunt Sarah's.

"Why don't ya come to church with me tomorrow?"
Dad asked, almost pleading. "Okay," I said.
I don't know why I agreed so easily.
Maybe after what I learned last night
from PCP, I needed a dose of church.
The next day, as we arrived at the service,
everyone was leaving. Church had ended.
"Crap! We forget to set the clocks ahead
for daylight savings time last night." I said.
"Yep, you're right. I'm so used to settin' them
ahead in the spring that I forgot this year
daylight savings time was in February.
Well, ya can go to church with me next week, then."

* * *

Part Eleven, High in My Mustang

I should probably put a *For Sale* sign
in my *Mustang's* window. But how can I?
It would be like selling my best friend.
I could get at least a thousand for it. But
it's not about the money. It's about hope,
hope that maybe one day I'll drive her again.
"After walking Ricky Henderson
and Dwayne Murphy in the sixth inning,
Earl Weaver has seen enough," Thompson says.
"He's replacing Palmer with Sammy Stewart.
The score remains tied at 2 runs apiece,
and we'll be right back after a word
from our sponsor," Thompson blasts from his booth.

"It's about time ya got back from the store.
What, did ya get lost or somethin'?" I joke,
as Jenny sinks into my bucket seat.
"Here! Take your *Doritos*. Why do ya do *that*?"
She demands. "Whaddya mean?" I ask.
"When I hand ya stuff, ya rarely respond."
"I don't always pay attention, I guess."
"Well, pay attention! It's annoyin'," she squawks.
"Here. Load up the bong. Will ya?" I say,
while handing over the paraphernalia.
After Jenny fills the six chambers with weed,
she grabs the Bic from my shirt pocket and lights
one up, and another right after it.
"That's good stuff," Jenny says, coughing through her nose,

her smile returning to her sweaty face.
"Ya look like ya feel better, now," I say.
"Here," she says, handing the bong back to me.
When I take it from her hand, I say, "See,
I'm payin' attention this time." She giggles,
while grabbing us both a beer from my cooler.
As I choke down two more hits from the bong,
she silences the O's game and slips
some Eagles to nest in the 8-track player.
Reclining back in the seat a bit to rest,
after she twisted up the volume to "Life
in the Fast Lane," I am reminded of
the time I wrecked my '66 Ford *Fairlane*,
on Thanksgiving 1977.
Oh boy! Angels were emptying out buckets
of mop water on Pasadena that day.
And with broken windshield wipers, I was stuck,
like a lunatic in bedlam, until
my best friend, *Budweiser*, and I solved
the problem by attaching a piece of string
to each wiper blade and running it through
the driver's-side and passenger's-side windows.
I remember how satisfaction filled me,
while I drove and powered the wipers
with this contraption of twine in my right hand,
while steering with my left hand, resting
my right hand only long enough to grab
and to gulp the *Budweiser* by my side.
When I turned onto Hickory Point Road,
I plugged in a favorite driving song,

"Let it Ride," by Bachman-Turner Overdrive,
and gave the engine a little extra juice,
until I noticed a car backing out
of its driveway. And, so, I bore down
on my brake pedal and spun out of control,
slamming passenger's-side first into a tree.
When a lady asked me if I was okay,
all I could say was, "Did I kill anyone?"
"No, hun. The only thing you hit was this tree."
I felt instantly sobered and relieved.
Within minutes I learned that the car,
that had been backing out of the driveway,
belonged to the daughter of the pastor
at my father's church: Lake Shore Baptist.
The cop who arrived at the scene knew me well,
since he had already busted me before—
on a larceny charge for stealing a bike.
I think the pastor somehow persuaded
the policeman not to arrest me,
and I was fortunate because I was still
on probation from my last arrest.

Shortly after moving to Pasadena,
I started stealing bikes, and whatever else
I thought I could acquire through thievery.
One Sunday, at age 17, I walked
to the store for the sole purpose of
buying cigarettes, not to steal something.
But when I arrived and saw a kid park
his ten-speed bicycle in front of the store,

temptation called out to me, saying:
You can get forty bucks for that one. Take it!
So within minutes of snatching it,
and hiding it in the woods, a cop walked
into my backyard and arrested me.
After showing him where I ditched the bike,
he cuffed me and placed me in his cruiser,
while Mr. Ralph, a neighbor my dad had
been trying to win to Jesus Christ, seemed
to smirk as he witnessed a rebellious son
bring dishonor to his Godly father.
At least Mr. Ralph went to church *that* day,
even if it was only to find
my father, and to gloat while he told how
a cop took me away in handcuffs.

"Why aren't ya workin' today?" Jenny asks,
jerking me away from my foul memories.
"I felt like partyin', so I took off."
"Liar!" She squawks. "How can ya stand workin'
in that sweatshop with your ex's father?
Are ya masochistic or somethin', Matt?"
"Ya don't know what *masochistic* means, girl.
When did *you* start speakin' in ten-dollar words?"
"Shut up and answer me this, moron.
Do ya still see her there?" "Every day," I say.
"Ya still love her. I know ya do," she says.
"I gotta get this crap home to mom, before
she sends a search party out for me. Thanks
for the buzz. And the *Doritos* are on me."

"Yeah. Well, ya better wipe 'em off ya," I slur,
"Ya don't wanna mess up those *Levi's*, girl!"
"Oh! So now you're a comedian. Huh?
Very funny," she says, "Don't quit your day job.
No. I take that back. Ya need to quit *that* job!"
Why did she have to bring *her* up? Isn't
RP enough to deal with today,
without thinking about Janie Graber!

*   *   *

Part Twelve, Let's Fight

In the middle of the eleventh grade,
I started my fourth new school in just
over 2 ½ years. But this time,
I wasn't the only one changing schools.
Our whole class was moving into a brand
new one called Chesapeake Senior High.
By then, Pasadena had become a fit
for me, like a well-worn flannel shirt.
As I settled into its drug culture,
and relaxed pace, school became a place
I'd appear at only every so often.
On most visits, I was drunk, or stoned, or both,
yet my *blindness* still besieged these walls
of insobriety I hid behind,
while it knocked the mortar from them bit by bit.
Before one such visit to school, I had lost
count of how many shots of *Old Grand-Dad*
I had chugged with my friend, Jason Black. Boozing,
by then, had become a sport. And like
how a riding crop propels a horse along,
so, too, pride prodded my friends and me onward,
as we tried to outduel each other drinking.
Unfortunately, for me, and for those
around me, more times than not, drinking
reduced me to a quick-tempered lunatic.
And whatever thought popped into my head,
somehow, it got vomited out of my mouth.

And such was the case when Jason drove us
to school that morning. We arrived late, and,
when I entered my fourth period math class,
I dropped my head to the desk for a snooze.
Mrs. Morehead summed up her displeasure,
when she banged her fist on my desk and said,
"No one, Mr. Harris, sleeps in my class."
Her condescending tone triggered these words:
"Here's the common denominator!
If ya weren't so borin', Mrs. Morehead,
no one would be noddin' off in your class."
Amid oohs, laughter, and whistles from the room,
Mrs. Morehead threw my butt out of her class.
As I sat in the administrator's room,
she kept asking me if I'd been drinking,
and every time she asked, I said, "No, I swear."
And though the grape bubble gum I gnawed on
helped mask the alcohol on my breath a bit,
I am certain my eyes betrayed my lie.
Everyone told me how they turned a deep red,
whenever I partied. So because she
didn't know exactly what to do with me,
or, perhaps, she was trying to protect me,
she sent me home in a taxi cab.

Later that afternoon, at The Park,
I met up with Auggie Bell, and said, "I heard
Sonny Roberts hit on your gal, Annie."
"Yeah, and it's not the first time. I'm gonna
whoop up on him. We're supposed to get it straight

right here at 4:00. Ya wanna back me up?
Nathan Carlyle promised to pitch in, too,
but as usual he'll probably be late."
"Why not, I ain't been in a brawl for awhile."
I'd soon regret my decision. Sure enough,
right at 4:00, Sonny and his friend, Donny Shores,
swaggered up to us, as Auggie greeted them,
"Hey, look, Matt, it's Sonny and Cher. Why don't ya
sing 'I Got You Babe' to each other?"
With that, Sonny shoved Auggie, and then fists
began to fly between the two, while Donny
and I just stood there and looked at each other.
I suddenly didn't want to be there.
But before I could decide what to do,
Donny broke the silence and said to me,
"What's your problem, moron?" "I take care
of my problems. What's yours, sea Shores," I barbed.
I don't know if I would have seen it or not,
even if I would have had perfect vision.
But after his right fist crashed into my nose,
and although my knees buckled a bit,
we both were surprised I was still standing.
My nose bled like a ketchup bottle
in a glutton's hands at a French-fry feast.
While white specks floated in front of my eyes,
like tiny insects fluttering about,
I told myself, *Don't let him hit ya again.*
If he did, I knew he'd knock my butt out.
The battle seemed to slow and became distant.
Dad always told me, *if ya fight, fight to win.*

So I used my feet at first and kept my head
out of the way. I kicked him in the torso
and the knees, though I was aiming for his groin.
After landing a couple of punches,
I got him in a headlock and bled
all over his back. By then, I saw
Sonny and Auggie standing by watching us.
After about ten minutes Donny and I
had had about enough for one day.
After everyone left, I sat on the ground,
weary and woozy, wondering how
in the world to stop my nose from bleeding.

Several weeks later, as I worked my shift,
at the Royal Farm Store, I wondered how long
it would take for customers to ask me,
after I had already rung them up,
Did you get the Coke, or the gum, or the chips?
The honest ones were being helpful, I knew.
But it was still embarrassing to miss
ringing up items right in front of me.
Sure, I would see some of them but not all.
The more incompetent I felt the more
numb I became to the world around me.
By then, I'd been working at the store
for months as a cashier and a stock boy.
But I enlarged the borders of my billfold
by practicing the art of embezzlement.
As I grew older, a mindset developed,
like a vine twisting around my thinking,

that I was entitled to take what I pleased.
And to everyone else in society,
catch me if ya can was my challenge to them.

As the night wore on, Janie Graber,
and one of her friends, dropped in to buy some stuff.
Janie lived right down the street from the store,
and when she visited, which was frequently,
we flirted and exchanged pleasantries.
"Did you get the *Mound's Bar*, Matt?" Janie asked,
after I had rung up her soda and smokes,
but oblivious to her candy bar,
sitting in plain view next to her soda can.
"No. I forgot, sorry," I said sheepishly.
"No need to be sorry," she cooed in a way
that seemed to make everything all right.
And even my bad eyes could see how she
moved with great prowess toward the front door.
I knew it was probably wishful thinking
to even consider that her visits
might in some way be ostensible
for her to come in and talk with me.

Erase those thoughts from your head right now, ya jerk,
I ordered myself. *She's trouble. After all,*
she has had a boyfriend for several years.
And besides, she was not only friendly
with you but with everyone else as well.

And yet how was I able to resist

the way she carried her scrawniness,
or batted those puppy dog eyes at me,
or that wisp of stray, dark hair that more often
than not danced on her cheek below her left eye,
or her sweet words, as they poured out through
a smile revealing a slight overbite,
that punctuated her face with uniqueness?
No weapons of war could withstand that battle!
It was as if she was the sea's bottom,
and someone tied cinder blocks to my legs
and hurled me into the ocean's depths.

The next day, in the smoking area,
at school, Janie grabbed my arm and said,
"Hey, Matt, give me a light. You forgot
to give me matches yesterday, when I bought
my smokes. I'm going to tell your boss," she teased.
"You're gonna get me fired, girl, and then who's
gonna only charge ya for a small coffee
when ya buy a large one," I reminded.
"Then just don't let it happen again, mister,"
she smiled, as she sauntered down the walkway.

Not long after my brawl with Donny Shores,
we gained mutual respect for each other,
and became friends and ate lunch together,
whenever I paid a visit to school.
And on those occasions, Janie Graber
and her friend, Katie Latzman, also joined us.
During lunchtime one day, while we laughed,

flirted and kidded around, as we chowed down
our pork 'n' beans and cold cut submarines,
a substance splattered on the side of my face.
I heard laughter from the table beside us,
as I wiped off the glob of mayonnaise
from my cheek. Jocks, probably showing off
for Katie and Janie, had hit their mark.
And I hit mine, when I catapulted
a spoonful of beans amid their huddle.
Janie choked on her milk, as she laughed mid-gulp,
while Donny looked at me and said, "Uh-oh!"
Katie excused herself for the ladies' room.
Jocks hated long-haired potheads like me,
who wore sleeveless jean jackets with phrases
of self-expression etched ever so
poetically on our backs like the one
emblazoned on mine: *Born to be Wild*.
Tit for tat, I thought. And that was that.
As I headed for the smoking area,
I lit my cigarette and leaned against
the outside glass to the cafeteria.
"Why did you hit me with pork 'n' beans, punk?"
Craig Myerson asked, as I blew smoke
from my *Salem* in his face, and said,
"Someone threw mayo in my face first, jock strap!"
What outcome would a scientist predict
if a two-hundred-pound linebacker type punched
a one-hundred-forty-pound warrior poet?
Extreme pain, probably, and lots of blood?
Not necessarily. When he planted

his first punch, just below my left eye,
it sat me on the cement for a second.
As I cleared my head, and mustered courage,
I sprang to my feet, while Craig just laughed
and belted me in the forehead. Undaunted,
I felt nothing but adrenaline-fueled
fury, as I peppered him with punches
to the face and body. I was quick enough
not to let the oaf grab me. I did not want
this to turn into a wrestling match.
"What are ya doin'? Get off me!" I hollered,
as two teachers collared me from behind.
Craig lunged toward me. And I jumped up
and kicked him in the throat, freeing myself
from my captors. I pursued Craig again,
when suddenly I tasted cement,
as my face impacted the concrete,
when, Mr. Jensen, our gym teacher,
grappled me to the ground from behind.
Our bout earned us a five-day vacation;
and after my suspension ended,
I returned to school and received this advice
from a kid who stopped me in the hallway:
"The next time you get into a fight,
why not pick on someone your own size?"

*   *   *

Part Thirteen, Comfortably Numb

Why can't I get my butt outta this *Mustang?*
It's not like it's fastened to the seat,
more like my motivation has been bled out,
staining the carpet of my ambition.
I have no desire to deal with blindness;
it's like a belt that binds my inner being,
strangling the energy that tries to escape.
What will I do? I am already losing
my ability to function at work.
I've fractured my left hand twice in six months,
while punching out bolt holes in asbestos
gaskets with a hammer and a punch.
Our bosses say the asbestos won't hurt us,
since it's *compressed.* But what about when
we cut it and dust flits in the air like gnats?
I can look forward to white lung, I suppose.
At least it takes decades for it to surface.
Janie Graber, maybe I still do love ya,
even though ya belong to another now.
I'll let *Budweiser* take that pain away,
even if it is just for a moment.

"We're in the top half of the eighth, still tied
at 2, with Rick Dempsey at bat, while Rich
Dauer awaits in the on-deck circle,"
Chuck Thompson voices through the AM static.
"Dempsey takes ball one from Rick Langford,
who's fanned eight batters so far," Thompson adds.

"Dempsey lines one into right-center field
for a base hit, his second of the day."
Come on Dauer get a hold of one.
Let's put this game away already!

"Do ya like talkin' to yourself, Matt?
Ya know what? You're the easiest person
to sneak up on," Jenny says, as she stands
next to my driver's-side window. "Oh,
there they are," she says, reaching across me
to grab her cigarettes from my console.
"I just bought some hash from Tony Gleason,"
she says, "Ya wanna smoke some? Or am I
interruptin' your baseball game?" She asks.
Before I have a chance to answer,
she marches in front of my car, while
en route to my passenger's-side seat.
After replacing the ballgame with Pink Floyd,
she loads her bowl with blond hash and fires it up,
her face contorting from a croup-like cough,
while expelling smoke. She passes it my way.

Four years ago, Tony Gleason and I
stole his mother's Volkswagen one evening,
neither of us having had a license yet.
After hours of drinking and riding
around, Tony collided dead center
into an oak tree on one of the trails
everyone liked to party on in the woods.
My head knocked the windshield onto the hood,

while my knees dented the glove compartment.
I suffered cuts, bruises, and a concussion.
The steering wheel knocked some of Tony's teeth out.
Fortunately, his mother did not press
charges. And since I was already on
probation, it kept me out of jail.
That was the first of eight car accidents
I would participate in, during
a two-year span. Four involved my own cars,
and four I was with friends while they wrecked theirs.
Blindness and intoxication don't mix well.
"Hey, Jenny, this hash is just what the doctor
ordered. I have become *comfortably numb.*

* * *

71

Part Fourteen, Driving Blind

On the first day of my senior year,
I drove my white Ford *Fairlane* to school.
It was a *beater* but was paid for in full
from the funds I'd saved from working and thieving.
Though I failed many tests I should have passed,
the one I should have failed I passed: my eye test
at the MVA for my driver's license.
For months, prior to passing my driver's test,
percussion from two questions kept resounding
over and over again in my mind, while
worries sandwiched themselves between their impact:
Could I even see well enough to drive?
If not, wouldn't the MVA find out?
Since it was every young man's dream to drive,
I pursued my goal with tunnel vision,
both literally and figuratively.
I failed the first test without ever
realizing I had sped through the stoplight.
"Pull over and put the car in park, son,"
the driving instructor commanded me.
After a month of beating myself up,
for either being too stupid or too blind—
I didn't know which to blame for my failure—
I advanced a little further through the course,
during my second test, until I backed in
to a wall, while attempting a three-point turn.
By the time I readied for my third attempt,
the test course was etched into my memory.

I received my driver's license without
any restrictions at all for my eyes.
That meant my *blindness* was all in my head. Right?
Maryland wouldn't issue a license
to a kid with poor eyesight. Would they?
My driver's license only addled my brain,
as more doubts about my sanity surfaced.
And, yet, whenever I drove at nighttime,
I never ventured into unfamiliar
surroundings because I could not see to drive
on roads without a double-yellow line,
which I used as a guide to keep me on track.
I knew that under no circumstance
should I ever remotely consider
driving through the Baltimore Harbor Tunnel.
When I'd ridden as a passenger through it,
my eyes would instantly enter *timeout* mode.
And they readjusted to it only when
we were about to exit the channel,
1½ miles later, just in time
for my eyes to enter their *whiteout* phase,
as we resurfaced into daylight.

Midway through the first semester of twelfth grade,
I partied just about every day.
While sipping *Old Grand-Dad*, gulping *Budweisers*,
and smoking weed and PCP, my descent
into self-extinction only quickened.
By Halloween, I was failing every course;
and since I needed to pass all my classes

to graduate in 1978,
I went AWOL from Chesapeake High School.
And, so, like a cook who slings hash on a grill,
I slung my education on the scrap heap.

By Christmas, I had mustered enough courage
to ask Janie Graber out for a date.
And to my surprise, she said, "Of course."
Janie Graber was not in my league at all;
besides her beauty, she was smart and rich.
Her father owned a machine shop and lavished
Janie with a comfortable lifestyle.
I would have loved to have taken her out
to a movie or to dinner alone
in my own car. But since my driving skills
proved unsteady, even when I was sober,
I needed to devise a plan quickly
that did not include me behind the wheel.
My *blindness* was NOT going to mess this up.
That evening at home I called my old friend,
Jeeter Jones, from Lakeland, and set up
a double date with him and Janie's friend,
Katie Latzman, along with Janie and me.
On Saturday evening, we picked up the girls
in Jeeter's Ford *Pinto* at Janie's house.
Against my argument to the contrary,
Jeeter brought along a quarter pound of weed
to sell and to smoke. The girls wanted to see
Saturday Night Fever, but, by the time we
arrived at the theater, we decided

instead to keep stoking our buzzes,
heightened already by the falling snow,
which added to the remains of a storm
that had pummeled Pasadena days before.

As soon as we entered Fort Smallwood Park—
a stronghold the U.S. once used to protect
the entrance to The Baltimore Harbor, but
by 1977 had become
a popular hangout for partiers—
an unplowed trail became an overnight stall
for the *Pinto* as its hooves spun helplessly.
"Jeeter, where did ya learn to drive, ya moron?"
I scolded, as he mercifully replaced
The Bee Gees with *Who's Next*, by The Who.
Luckily, we had just restocked the *Pinto*
with beer and burgers from McDonalds.
"Jeeter, where's your common sense? If the cops come,
and find that weed I told ya *not* to bring,
we're all gonna get busted. And I'm still . . ."
Janie interrupted me with a tug on
my jacket sleeve as if to say *let it go,*
and then stole a hearty bite from my burger.
"Bon Appetite, ya Hamburglar," I said.
What a dull-witted thing to say, I thought.
Even though sincerity laced her giggle,
I wished I could had seen her face right then.
As Jeeter lost himself in *Teenage Wasteland*,
Katie became more nippy toward him than
the brittle breeze shaking our *Pinto*, that blew

from across the Patapsco River.
At least the *Pinto's* heater worked well, keeping
us toasty inside our metal ice box
throughout the night. Janie and I talked
easily about our lives and dreams.
One of her goals was to become Honored Queen
in an organization called Job's Daughters,
which was connected with the masons somehow.
What a classy girl I remembered thinking,
so different from other girls I'd dated.
Janie slept with her head on my shoulder, till
the sun rose and a fellow with a snowplow
helped scoop us out of our predicament.
When we took Janie home her father was
wide-eyed and waiting in the driveway.
He did not believe for one minute
that we were marooned in a snowdrift all night.
And though Janie's father wanted to choke me
for keeping his daughter out all that night,
weeks later he still offered me a job,
after Janie highly recommended me,
to work at his machine shop in Baltimore.

One of my tasks at Graber's Machine Shop was
to unload trucks when materials arrived.
Physically, this was not a problem for me;
but visually, I was presented with
a challenge, of course. Whenever I went
from inside to outside and vice versa,
timeout and *whiteout* hindered my movement.

While these obstacles ping ponged back and forth,
and with diminished peripheral vision,
I practically unloaded these trucks blind,
which created a great deal of stress for me,
a pain in which I endured alone.
Even though Janie and I had become close,
I never shared my *blindness* with her.
How could I? I didn't know what it was!
And, yet, turmoil swelled inside me for not
having told her about this secret.
I didn't know how to explain it and thought
she might not love me anymore if I tried.
Drugs only brought me temporary relief.
And since I'd been with Janie, I curtailed
my drug use but increased my drinking.
Even though I worked with several guys,
I still felt forsaken and lost in the shop.
And since I seemed to be using my hearing
more and more to aid my failing eyesight,
my *blindness* seemed to worsen whenever
the noise level from machinery increased.
And because I dated the boss' daughter,
I wanted to work hard for Mr. Graber,
but believed my efforts went unnoticed,
which only added to my frustration.

Even while my driving skills declined,
I still spent much of my free time with Janie.
Since I drank most days, Janie agreed to drive,
even though she didn't have a license yet.

She loved driving my car, and I loved drinking.
So I kept drinking, and Janie kept driving,
which unriddled my driving dilemma.

A page soon turned in our relationship, when,
after dinner one night, the phone rang. "Hello,"
I answered. It was Janie. "What's up?" I asked,
and don't tell me heaven like ya always do."
"Will you come over and pick me up?
We need to talk," she said grimly. *Uh-oh,*
I thought, as I said, "I'll be right over."
She met me in her driveway, as I pulled in.
"What's the matter?" I asked. "Just drive," she ordered,
while getting into the passenger's-side seat.
Tears can never be a good sign, I thought,
as she cried while I drove to Fort Smallwood Park,
where we could talk uninterrupted.
"I'm pregnant, Matt. Two months." She told me,
as soon as I turned off the ignition.
A frightful chill wrapped its arms around me,
like it was December, rather than June.
I hugged her and felt warmth, but still wished
I had stopped at the liquor store, before
ever even having picked Janie up.
"I wanted to become Honored Queen
at Job's Daughters. I was next in line," she cried.
"But Honored Queens are supposed to be virgins.
Since pregnancy opposes their moral code,
if I keep this baby, I'm disqualified."
"*If* ya keep the baby? What do ya mean, *if*?

78

A life is more important than some club!
Please, Janie, tell me ya believe that, too.
All I know is that I love ya and want this
baby. We can get married. And I can start
workin' my way up in your dad's company."
I won't let my blindness mess that up,
I promised myself, as Janie said,
"You're right, Matt. But my parents think otherwise.
You know how involved my father is
with the masons and how important
the status of Honored Queen is to him."
"But it's hypocritical, Janie!
Can't ya see that? Even if ya weren't
pregnant, you're still not a virgin. And *that*
fact alone disqualifies ya anyway."
"Yeah, but what they don't know won't hurt 'em.
And besides, my parents think I'm too young,
so they want me to get an abortion.
I'm so scared and confused and never told you
that I had an abortion last year,
right after I broke up with Chucky.
And I'm afraid if I have another one,
I won't be able to conceive again."
That *chill* just wrapped its arms around me tighter
than a Michelin hugs an auto's rim,
as I sat quietly for a moment,
while soaking up this new revelation,
like kitty litter absorbing cat pee!
Had she aborted her other baby
to maintain her status of "purity"

for this club I now hated: Job's Daughters?
Only if I had a Budweiser right now,
I thought to myself. *Think, before ya speak!*
"Look, sweetheart," I said, "The past is the past.
Let's get married and have this child together.
We've already talked about marriage.
We'll just wed sooner rather than later."
"How 'bout October," she said, as she kissed me.
But her mind soon turned on the matter, quicker
than a weather change on Chesapeake Bay,
when she decided to abort our baby,
claiming her parents had insisted on it.
I told her I wanted no part of that,
and the blood of our baby was on *her* hands!

*   *   *

Part Fifteen, Infanticide

"Ya know what, Jenny? I wish I had the cash
to get this bad boy back on the road again.
Whaddya doin'? Oh, snorin'. I guess
between the hash, the weed, and the booze,
it's no surprise you're takin' a snooze.
That bucket seat's rather comfortable, huh?"

It's bubblin'; it's bubblin'; my bong keeps bubblin'!

As more weed scratches the itch in my lungs,
my memories unleash themselves on me;
these beasts lash out at my mind with thorny claws,
taunting me about my RP, and how
Roe v. Wade aided and abetted in
state sanctioned infanticide of my baby.
I guess to try and cheer my sorry butt up,
some friends told me how lucky I was not
to have had to pay for Janie's abortion
like some of them had to pay for their girlfriends'.
For me, it was never about money.
It was about principle. How could I pay
that *hit man*, with M.D. behind his name,
to suck the life from my own flesh and blood?

*   *   *

Part Sixteen, Busted Again

Soon after Janie *murdered* our baby,
two acronyms had taken me captive:
LSD and *PCP* enlightened
my unlit regions with a deeper darkness
than *Budweiser* or weed could ever offer.
Dang, Danny Dumas, late again! I complained
to myself, my patience evaporating,
like smoke emanating from an exhaust pipe,
as I waited at The Park for him
and Auggie Bell to arrive with my hit
of acid they promised to bring to me.
Danny had supposedly scored some
butt kickin' acid called *Red Dragon*.
I'm ready to slay it if he ever gets here.

"You're later than a pregnant girl's period,"
I told Danny, after fifteen more minutes
had passsed, as he and Auggie stopped beside me.
"Eat a cat turd and die!" Danny countered.
"If you still want the *Red Dragon*, get in."
"Will ya turn the light on, Danny," I asked,
climbing into the backseat of his *Vega*.
"I'd like to see what the heck I'm buyin'.
What's up, Auggie?" I said, as he looked at me,
stone faced, from the front passenger's-side seat.
"Here's a beer for ya, Matt," Auggie offered.
"Thanks," I said, as I grabbed the opened can.
Auggie never offers anyone a beer,

so why would he give me one, opened even?
Stop being so paranoid, I told myself.
As Danny gave me a hit of *Red Dragon*,
he said, "Keep your money. It's on the house."
What's up with all the kindness? I wondered,
till Auggie hollered above The Rolling Stones,
"Can we turn the dang light off now, girls?"
That's more like it. I thought. *Back to normal!*
As I placed the small papered square piece
of acid on my tongue, and chased it
with lukewarm *Budweiser*, Danny sped off
to a shopping center where we partied.
Within an hour, dozens of people
had mustered to get high in the parking lot.
I had dropped acid dozens of times before,
but this time was different from all the rest.
It booked me on a flight I could not cancel,
as that *Dragon* breathed his demonic flame.
And when, like an arsonist, he ignited
the walls of my sanity with his torch,
I saw sounds, while people taunted me and said,
It's time for you to die now, Matt. Kill him!
Kill him! It's time for you to die now, Matt!
I saw a police car pull in and thought, *Great!*
He won't let them kill me. I'm safe now.
But another teenager stepped out
and joined in with the crowd's mantra and said,
It's time for you to die now, Matt. Kill him!
Kill him! It's time for you to die now, Matt!
More voices I saw said, *Here comes the good part.*

83

As the *Dragon* continued his ascent
from his lair, maniacal laughter pierced
through my pores like hypodermic needles,
infusing fiendish tremors through my body.
I wrested myself from the madness, and, yet,
it trailed behind me, like a wagon
hitched to my back filled with delirium.
I felt like a phantom roller skating,
without skates, up Mountain Road, dodging cars,
whose headlights seemed so close I could touch them
without any physical consequences.
I finally arrived at the Farm Store,
my former place of employment. As I stormed
through the doors, the activity inside
massacred my mind with stimulation,
while refrigeration from soda coolers
roared like an eighteen-wheeler. Inside the store,
the lighting seemed to separate into shreds,
while customers stared at me with strange masks.
I needed a dose of night, so I left
and staggered down Janie's darkened street.
As if a demon directed my feet,
I stumbled into parked cars, while lights, beaming
from porch lamps and front windows, escorted
my footsteps toward my former girlfriend's house.
A car, meanwhile, stopped and a man said, "Matt,
is that you? What's wrong?" It was my father.
"Come on, Matt, get in the car. Hurry up!"
Yet, I was not convinced it was him, until
the sound from his *Galaxie's* engine

persuaded me. And only then I got in.
A woman, who knew me from the Farm Store,
called my dad, warning him I was in trouble.
And, later, as I entered through my front door,
my skin felt like it was slipping off.
In my head, I believed I had died.
When a fiend usurped my soul from my body,
he brought me to the gates of Hades, where
I saw myself in a casket, my fingers
folded as if in prayer. At the viewing,
my mother clasped my cold hands. As she wept,
I hovered above the coffin and hollered:
"I'm not dead, mom. I'm right here," as I touched
her shoulder trying to console her distress.
She did not acknowledge me at all,
as she clutched the still hands of her *dead* son.

A couple of months after my *death,*
Danny Dumas drove me and Auggie Bell
to Annapolis so Auggie could sell
baggies of flakes manufactured in hell.
As "Renegade," by Styx, branded our ears with

The jig is up, the news is out. They
finally found me. The renegade
who had it made retrieved for a bounty.
Never more to go astray. This'll be
the end today of the wanted man,

Danny turned the wrong way onto Taylor

Avenue. A guardrail on its shoulder stood
in its stance, like Dallas' Doomsday defense
positioned on the line of scrimmage,
ready to sack our four-wheeled quarterback.
Horns blew from cars, instead of from the band,
while Firestones screeched rather than applause from fans.
The back of the front passenger's seat halted
my momentum, and, like a lineman, forced me
to fumble my pipe brimming with *PCP*.
On the wrong side of Taylor Avenue,
beneath a flickering Bic butane,
my Timex still ticking read 2:10 a.m.
I was stoned with a brain that crackled,
like a fire log swallowed up by wretched flame,
as warnings sounded in my mind like sirens:
Toss the dope. Run, Matt, run! But toss my dope? Nope!
I don't think so! As I loitered at the wreck,
shackled in the shadows of dependency,
PCP and I had no grounds for divorce,
not even a chance for separation,
such were the bonds of my addiction.
I huddled with the team, as Annapolis
dispatched its team, adorned in badges and blue.
When the cell door slammed shut that night, I did not
know how soon it might open again.

*   *   *

Part Seventeen, Pleading My Case

"Baltimore defeats Oakland 4 to 2,
though they needed 12 innings to do it,"
Chuck Thompson exclaims from the radio.
At least they won, though I missed most of the game.
"Ya finally woke up, I see, sleepy head.
Did ya know ya snore like a chainsaw?"
"Shut up, moron! Did ya know I've been up
for ten minutes already and *you*
didn't even know it. What's up with that?
Not payin' attention again, Matt, huh?"
"Whaddya doin', Jenny?" I ask, puzzled.
"I'm writin' a check for ya. What's today's date?"
"It's August 21, 1981."
"It's for the $25.00 dollars ya loaned me
last month to help pay for my new tires."
"I don't take checks. Put it away, Jenny.
Besides, it wasn't a loan. It was a gift."
And then changing the subject, I say,
while handing over the unoccupied pipe,
"Here! Fill her up with some more hash, will ya?
I gotta find a tree. I'll be right back.
These *Budweisers* have gone right through me!"
While I was taking care of my business,
guilt jolted my conscience awake, when I saw
the Rhododendron bush by my side.
It was a Mother's Day present I stole
one day from a flower stand in Lakeland.
Wasted on Vodka and Valium, I staggered

over to the potted bush, snatched it up,
then looked right into the eyes of the guy,
who worked at overseeing the stand, and said,
"This belongs to my mom. Catch me if ya can."
Why I'm not in prison I'll never know.
When I get back, Jenny has the bowl cooking.
"I gotta get some of this hash from Tony."
"Do ya wanna play cards later?" Jenny asks.
"Maybe. But first, I gotta find Tony."
"Ya never miss work anymore. So why
did ya take off today?" Jenny asks
for the second time this afternoon.
Why does she keep asking me this? I wonder.
"I just needed some rest, I guess. Why?"
"It seems like somethin's botherin' ya, that's all."
Jenny is one of my best friends, but at times
she's more like a mother hen. It's nice, though,
to have a friend like her who cares so much.
"Nothin's botherin' me. Leave it alone!"
No way, I'm tellin' her about my blindness.
"Ya never should have gone back to Graber's, Matt."
"Believe me, darlin', when I tell ya,
I'm not gonna receive some gold watch
for havin' worked there for 25 years!
I wanna get out of that asbestos dump,
as soon as I can line somethin' else up.
Look, Jenny, after Janie, and that bad
acid trip, my drug bust, and everything else,
I needed some time to tune out alone,
to get my head screwed on straight again.

So after I got my act together,
if ya even wanna call it that,
I went back to work there because I needed
to redeem myself for messin' things up.
I was lucky Graber even took me back,
after all the crap that happened with Janie."
"He probably only took ya back because
he wanted ya to get back with Janie.
He knew ya were better than that moron
she finally married. What's his name, Marcel?
And what kinda mother names her kid *Marcel*?
And how long did *they* last? A year, wasn't it?"
For some reason, Jenny never liked Janie.
Janie knew it, too. I think it was because
Jenny had lived a rough life, while Janie's life,
at least materially, was lavish,
by Pasadena standards, anyway.

"If mom hadn't told ya about her lawyer,
that judge would have marinaded your butt,
then cooked it with a steep prison sentence."
"*Steep* might be an exaggeration, Jenny,
yet, one night in jail, though, was bad enough.
But if Auggie hadn't ditched those baggies,
bulging with *Satan Dust*, prison would have been
our home for a long, long time. Of course,
since they separated us in the jail
that night, after we were arrested,
I never knew, till they released us
the next day, that he had tossed the baggies,

before the cops came and hauled our butts away.
I assumed we had been busted for those, too.
I was so wasted then that nothing made sense.
As I sobered that night, a fear snagged me,
like sharp fish hooks biting through my skin
from the inside, that I'd be the county's house
guest for awhile. I'll never forget that night
two years ago in 1979."
"An angel must have been lookin' out for ya,
or some other higher power," Jenny says.
"I do believe God delivered me, somehow.
But for what reason? I have no clue."
"Here, Matt, take the bowl. I'm handin' it to ya."
"I think I've had enough for today, Jenny.
It makes me wanna quit usin' drugs,
when I think of the legal mess I got
myself into for chasin' after them.
I had never been more scared than the day
that I stood before that judge, who could have snatched
my freedom away from me for two years
for possessin' that PCP I refused
to toss, even though I had a chance to.
But in hindsight, it's clear to me now how
it possessed me more than I possessed it.
But after the judge dismissed my charges,
on a technicality, I was stunned.
And, at the same time, knowin' I was guilty,
the emotions I felt, I would wager, were
the exact opposite of someone
who had been wrongly convicted of a crime,

and sentenced to a lengthy prison sentence."
"I should've kicked Janie's butt for ya, Matt.
That would have been one bruised up Honored Queen,"
Jenny slurs, while shadowboxing my windshield.
"Don't be bustin' out my window, Sugar Ray.
That's the *Budweiser* talkin', girl," I say.
"I got your *Budweiser* right here," Jenny quips,
while smacking me in the side of the head.
"I'm so fast ya didn't even see it
comin'. Did ya, mister?" Jenny taunts.
If only ya knew, I think, with a smirk.

*   *   *

Part Eighteen, Saved by Grace

After I slammed the door to my *Mustang* shut
that night, on 8/21/81,
having mourned enough that day for my RP,
raindrops slid down my windshield like tears. And months,
later, tears slid down my face like raindrops, when
I learned how spiritual blindness plagued me, too:
a darkness painted black with the brush of sin.
But the Lord began to show me the ladder
on which I could climb out from my dark pit.
A darkness far worse than the kind RP
could had ever abandoned me in:
a darkness every human inherited
from the patriarch of our race, Adam,
who, while in the midst of Eden's splendor,
bit freely from fruit God had forbidden,
and, thus, left his legacy of death through sin,
that kidnapped us from our relationship
with our Father, who loved us so much He sent
the second Adam, Jesus, His Son, to pay
our ransom with the Divine Blood he shed
for all who will repent and call on His name.
After His Father raised Him from the dead,
that Light led multitudes of blind people's feet
onto the path of life everlasting.
I knew the Light was Jesus, who came to save,
yet I loved the darkness rather than the Light,
only because my deeds were evil.
In the eyes of God, whom I had offended,

all have sinned and fall short of His glory,
whether one is a soccer mom in the 'burbs,
or a prostitute working Baltimore street,
or a blind druggie from Pasadena.

O dreaded *Death* where shall we hide from you:
in the philosophies of this world,
or in the promises of politicians,
whether Democratic or Republican,
or in the theories of almighty science,
or in carousing, or in comfort foods, or
in a career, or perhaps a bank account,
or in a hobby, or in the cares of life,
or in the arms of a forbidden lover,
or even in the arms of one who's not,
or in watching sports, or in Romance Novels,
or behind a bong or bottle of booze? No!
Only the Blood of Jesus will secure
a place for us in heaven forevermore.

So when at last I listened to Scripture's call,
I read every *thine, thou,* and *thee* and every
who *begot* who, from Genesis Chapter One
to Matthew Chapter Ten, where Jesus said,
". . . Whoever confesses Me before men,
him I will also confess before
My Father who is in heaven. But
whoever denies Me before men, him
I will also deny before My Father
who is in heaven." These words of Jesus pierced

through my stronghold of cowardice that strangled
my heart: Fear that men might mock muted my mouth
from publicly proclaiming *Jesus is Lord!*
But, then, by grace, God gave this coward boldness
to declare to the night the name of Jesus.

On December 12, 1982,
I began my journey toward my Lord,
but later learned it was His Father, though,
who had been drawing me toward His Son.
On that Sunday morning, six inches of snow
blanketed earth like a polar bear's hide.
It was the day of my salvation. I knew.
Yet the enemy still fought for my soul,
so another battle warred in my mind,
stabbing it with stubbornness, as I thought:
If I get saved, then that proves my father's right.
(That fact my pride kept me from admitting to.)
Well then, I'll just go to another church!
Dad doesn't need to know if I get saved.
Was it any of his business anyway?
I'll go to Galilee Lutheran.
Since their service begins earlier than
Lake Shore Baptist's, I'll go there, get saved
and come home before dad ever gets back.
Proud of my plan, I lit up a *Salem*,
and shouldered my way through my front door.
Stepping out onto the ice-packed road,
flurries gathered swiftly on my hatless hair,
that danced a half-foot below my shoulders.

Bright-eyed with sobriety, at least for now,
I lumbered onward toward the church,
while peacefulness insulated my soul,
as the snow muffled the voices of children,
and the rudders of their sleds, while they steered
deftly between the trees, aligning their course,
that sloped toward a valley in the woods.

As soon as I set foot inside the door
of Galilee Lutheran Church, my eyes
entered into their familiar *timeout* mode,
as they transitioned to the indoor lighting.
Someone greeted me with a *good morning*;
and since I anticipated a handshake,
I extended mine and was surprised
by a church bulletin instead of a hand.
By the time my eyes cooperated,
the service had already begun,
so I stood amid a desolate pew,
as far from the pulpit as possible.
I didn't believe that I belonged there,
but said to myself, *I love ya Jesus,
but I don't know if I'll ever love church.*
Still, I threw in my voice with the rest of them,
and belted out songs from an ancient hymnal.
Something vexed my spirit while the pastor preached.
Come on! Come on! Get to the invitation,
I kept telling myself, eager to get saved.
With the last breath of the sermon breathed out,
the pastor closed with a word of prayer, and said,

"Thanks for coming out to worship with us
in the snow today. Have a safe trip home."
What! No invitation to get saved?
I felt the color fading from my face,
while panic filled my empty stomach.
"Ma'am," I said to a lady gathering
her belongings in the pew in front of me,
"I wanted to get saved today, ya know,
receive Christ as my Savior. Doesn't your church
have an altar call after the service?"
"We don't do anything like that here," she smiled.
"We're Lutheran." "Oh! All right, thank you," I said.

It felt as if my soul went a bit berserk,
as I bolted through the door of the church.
I feared my chance for salvation was doomed.
If I didn't get saved now, would I ever?
I knew if I hurried I'd still have time
to walk the quarter mile to Lake Shore Baptist.
The snowstorm greatly hindered my swiftness,
and my body was taut with tension,
as I slid along the side of Mountain Road,
praying none of these cars, that slithered
along the shifty roadway, would crush me,
before I received Christ as my Savior.
I had to pay closer attention because
the snow and ice distorted the normal sounds
of the street. And, since snow burdened the shoulders
of the road, I walked partly in the right lane.
Are churches allowed to close? I wondered.

If they do, I hope it's not today.
As I crossed through the slush-laden street,
frost bit at my body like a frothing dog.
While I skidded across the parking lot,
scraping sounds from a man shoveling snow bounced
from the bricks of the church. "Good morning," he said,
while steam flowed from his mouth like cigarette smoke.
"Hi! Hey, do they ever close church?" I asked.
"We wanted to close today. But the pastor
said he believed God wanted us opened.
So enjoy the service." "I will," I said.
Just before it started I slipped into
the pew closest to the back door. I spotted
mom and dad up front. I hoped they'd not see me.
Yet, suddenly, it did not matter to me
if they knew about my salvation or not.
I conceded right then that dad was right.
Still, I struggled but believed Jesus led me.
While battles bristled in my mind, doubts seethed
over with things God had already resolved.
As swords clashed inside me, vying for my soul,
Jesus flashed these words like neon through my mind:
"He who confesses Me before men him
I will also confess before my Father."

So I sang along with the congregation:

Just as I am, without one plea,
but that thy blood was shed for me,
and that thou bidst me come to thee,

97

O Lamb of God, I come, I come!

And when the pastor asked if any would like
to receive Jesus as their Savior,
with my heart focused solely on my Lord,
I sprang from my hellish ditch and dashed
down the aisle toward the front of the church.
"I wanna get saved, pastor," I cried out.
After a deacon named Wayne Foy walked over,
and greeted me with an angelic smile,
he lead me in a short prayer, in which I
repented from my sins and asked Jesus
to forgive me and to come into my life.
And at that moment, I was born again,
as God gave me His gift of eternal life.
It felt as if my soul had been swept clean
from the soot that collected there from my sin.

My parents, meanwhile, seemed stunned while they hugged me,
telling me my salvation was answered prayer.
"Do ya wanna ride home with us?" Mom asked.
"Nah, I'm gonna walk. But thanks anyway."
Mom and my sis had been saved just recently,
and, so, the entire Harris clan now knew Christ.
After I pushed my way through the church's door,
the man who had been shoveling snow said,
"I know why God wanted us to open now.
Welcome to the kingdom of God, son."
I nodded and smiled. As I headed for home,
relief diffused itself throughout my being,

like after having had an aching tooth pulled.
With the steady crunch of snow beneath my feet,
I neared my house when a soft voice whispered
from somewhere in the depths of my soul, saying:
"I want you to share Me in the darkness; and
marry a Christian woman." It was Jesus!
And, so, I responded to Him by saying,
"I don't know how to share Ya in the darkness,
but I'm willin' to try. And, Lord, Ya know
right now I don't know any Christian women!"

But that all changed after God cleaned me up,
and cured me from my drug-induced disease,
when He gifted me with Pamela's hand,
on whose finger I placed a wedding band,
with a cross enclosed inside a ring of love,
who since has blessed me with two cherubim:
our daughters, Julia and Abigail,
who know the Lord Jesus as their Savior, too.
And though I'm 99% blind now,
with a 60% hearing loss as well,
God's grace is still sufficient for me,
and His strength is made perfect through my weakness.
And over time God has shown me how to share
His Son in darkness through my poetry.
And, so, these four books I've written for my Lord:
*Poems On Some Parables Of Christ; Sonnets
for Messiah; Leaves of Prophecy;* and
Seeing Through Blindness, my poetic memoir.

Three decades, like a vapor, now have passed,
since God gave this blind man's heart some sight.
And those words Jesus once whispered to me,
after I received Him as my Savior,
on that snowy Sunday morning, way back
on December 12, 1982, still
lead me deeper into darkness to share
the Light of His salvation with the world. So
I've prayed that conviction of your sin will slice
steadily at your heart, until it turns
from stone to flesh and bleeds with understanding:
That where you will spend eternity, either
in heaven or in fiery hell, depends
on who you believe Jesus is—or isn't.
"For God so loved the world that He gave
His only begotten Son, that whoever
believes in Him should not perish but have
everlasting life" (John 3:16).
"For the wages of sin is death, but the gift
of God is eternal life in Christ
Jesus our Lord" (Romans 6:23).
Jesus, who never told a lie, once said,
"I am the resurrection and the life.
He who believes in Me, though he may die,
he shall live" (John 11:25).
Because God loves us He promises this:
"Everyone who calls on the name of
the Lord will be saved" (Romans 10:13).
Jesus paid the price to save our souls from hell.
And for every unsaved sinner, repentance

and belief are the two prerequisites.
Today is the day of salvation, so
if you're ready now to call on the name
of the Lord, and know for sure that you will have
a place in heaven with Christ Jesus,
then pray the prayer below, and mean it
in your heart. It's as simple as that!
I hope to see ya in God's Kingdom soon.

I have sinned against You, Lord, and need
forgiveness. Please forgive me of my sins
and come into my life. I confess
with my mouth that You, Jesus, are Lord.
I believe in my heart that You died
on the cross for my sins, and that God,
Your Father, has raised You from the dead.
I call on You, Jesus, for eternal life.
Help me, by Your kindness, to turn from my sin
and live for You forevermore. Amen!

* * *

"Therefore, if anyone *is* in Christ, *he is* a new creation; old things have passed away; behold, all things have become new" (2 Corinthians 5:17).